A STUDY GUIDE FOR

THE CHINESE

ADAPTING THE PAST / FACING THE FUTURE

Thomas M. Buoye

Center for Chinese Studies ♦ University of Michigan

Published by Center for Chinese Studies
The University of Michigan
Ann Arbor, Michigan 48109-1290

First Edition 1992
Second Printing 1994
Third Printing 1996

Printed and made in the United States of America

♾ The paper used in this publication meets the minimum requirements of the American National Standard for Information Sciences—Permanence of Paper for Publications and Documents in Libraries and Archives ANSI/NISO/Z39.48—1992.

ISBN 0-89264-104-5

Contents

Note to the Student

The Chinese: Adapting the Past, Facing the Future is an unusual textbook. The editors have chosen to introduce contemporary China through an array of readings that includes cultural source materials, historical documents, scholarly articles, even stories and poems. The result is a massive book that in some degree reflects the complexity and variousness of China itself. At the same time, as a compendium of diverse materials and often differing opinions, *The Chinese* presents a challenge to students accustomed to more conventional texts.

This *Study Guide* has been designed to help two kinds of students meet this challenge. For those who use *The Chinese* as a stand-alone classroom text, the *Study Guide* will help them integrate and assimilate the diverse materials and opinions they encounter in its pages. For other, nontraditional, students, this guide performs the additional service of coordinating the readings with the twenty-six half-hour video segments of *The Chinese* telecourse package. Students of both kinds will find the *Study Guide* helpful as they seek to consolidate their understanding of the many complex issues they will encounter. The editors' Introductions provide context and perspective; the *Study Guide* provides strategies for assimilating and retaining the most essential points. Neither can be used as a substitute for careful study of the readings themselves.

The organization of the *Study Guide* follows that of *The Chinese,* with six Parts—History and Geography, Politics, The Economy, Society, Culture, and The Future—subdivided into a total of thirteen Units. Each Unit in the *Study Guide* has the following components: First, there is a list of the pertinent readings and video segments, accompanied by a set of *Learning Objectives.* An *Overview* then summarizes the readings and relates them to each other and to the video segments, and a glossary of *Key Concepts* highlights major ideas and clarifies unfamiliar terms. The Unit concludes with *Review Questions* to help students test their grasp of the factual content of individual readings. At the end of each of the six Parts, students will find *Essay/Discussion Questions* requiring them to synthesize what they have learned and demonstrate comprehension of its larger significance.

Students may find different ways of using the *Study Guide,* but the following approach is sure to prove effective. For each Unit:

1) Read the *Learning Objectives,* the *Overview,* and the *Key Concepts*
2) Watch the video (telecourse students) and read the relevant selections in *The Chinese*
3) Reinforce what you have learned by rereading the *Overview* and *Key Concepts*
4) Answer the *Review Questions,* referring to the readings as necessary
5) Reexamine the *Learning Objectives* to make sure these goals have been achieved
6) Answer the appropriate *Essay/Discussion Questions* orally or in writing, using the guidelines to help you structure your response.

* * *

Many different systems have been used over the years for rendering Chinese words and names in the roman alphabet. The system currently used in most English-language scholarship and journalism is *pinyin,* officially endorsed by the People's Republic. It is the system used in this *Study Guide,* in the editors' Introductions in *The Chinese,* and in many of the readings. However, much literature on China employs the older Wade-Giles system, still used by some scholars and in a number of the readings in *The Chinese.* While students of China quickly learn that "Mao Zedong" and *Daodejing* (pinyin) are the same as "Mao Tse-tung" and *Tao Te Ching* (Wade-Giles), the different forms can be confusing. The appendices to this *Study Guide* contain both a Pinyin

Pronunciation Guide and a complete Pinyin/Wade-Giles Conversion Chart. Finally, the spellings of certain names, like "Confucius" and "Peking," belong to neither system but have become traditional in English.

Prologue

Video: "Reform in Crisis: The Aftermath of Tiananmen"

Hosted by CNN China correspondent Mike Chinoy, the video "Reform in Crisis" brings together a panel of China experts to examine the events that have occurred in China since the *Heart of the Dragon* series was first produced. When the videos that constitute the core of the course were filmed, China appeared to have embarked on a successful reform program. Within China and abroad, the mood was optimistic. By the late 1980s, however, it was apparent that reform had some unwanted and unanticipated side-effects. "Reform in Crisis" addresses the social, political, and economic problems created during the decade of reform, as well as the tragic events that ended in the Tiananmen Massacre on June 4, 1989.

As Martin Whyte notes, by the late 1980s both supporters and opponents of reform were dissatisfied. On the one hand, the reforms of that decade had not fulfilled the expectations of the students, intellectuals, and private entrepreneurs who had enthusiastically supported them. Although many Chinese prospered under the reforms, it was also clear that individuals with "connections" to powerful leaders benefited more and, most felt, benefited unfairly. Simultaneously, many government bureaucrats and Party cadres perceived the reforms as a direct threat to their political power and economic well-being. For example, price inflation, an unwanted side-effect of market reforms, had reached double digits in 1988 and was particularly harsh on government bureaucrats with fixed salaries. According to Martin Whyte, the educated youths, intellectuals, and private entrepreneurs who had expected to benefit from reform most were disillusioned by the political corruption, while government bureaucrats and Party cadres, who were predisposed to resist reform, felt the sting of inflation more severely. Faced with increasing political and social tensions, China's leaders hesitated and the reforms stalled.

In retrospect, the flaws of the reform effort are apparent. From the outset China's leaders had approached reform cautiously. Economically, market forces were permitted to play a larger role in the economy, but centralized economic planning was never completely dismantled. Politically, central control was relaxed, but the ultimate authority of the Party remained unquestioned. As Steven Goldstein notes, the partial nature of the reforms was indicative of the ambivalence of China's leaders. When the reform process bogged down and China's leaders faced tough choices, their indecisiveness prevented innovative responses and exacerbated political disagreements.

As discontent over the direction of the reforms mounted, splits developed within the leadership and between the people and the government. When the former Communist Party Secretary Hu Yaobang, a proponent of political as well as economic reform, died in April of 1989, Chinese students had taken to the streets to show their respect for Hu and their support for reform. What began as a demonstration in memory of Hu Yaobang proved to be the beginning of the prodemocracy movement. This was not the first time in modern Chinese history that students took to the streets to challenge the government. Prior to the death of Hu Yaobang, university students were preparing demonstrations to commemorate the seventieth anniversary of the May Fourth Movement (see Part 1, below). As China's leaders responded indecisively, the political demonstrations gained broader support. Clearly the student-led movement had tapped a reservoir of popular discontent. Similarly, the dilatory response of the Chinese government was indicative of the divisions within the ruling elite.

As we see in the video, political tensions reached a deplorable denouement in Tiananmen Square in the summer of 1989. Tragically, Chinese leaders ultimately chose to use military force to suppress popular demonstrations in Beijing and other cities. The brutality of the crackdown shocked the world and silenced dissent for the time being.

Interestingly, although the reform movement has been dealt a severe setback, the current leadership has not attempted to undo the existing reforms. As Rhoads Murphey observes, since the nineteenth century China has witnessed a variety of efforts at political and economic reform. History supplies examples of both success and failure, and it remains to be seen whether the events of 1989 marked the end of an era or a temporary setback in China's ongoing struggle to reform and modernize.

Part 1

History and Geography

Part 1 introduces the historical and geographic factors that provide keys to understanding the China of today—and tomorrow. Highlighting some of the major developments in Chinese history from 2000 B.C. to the present, this section of the course focuses on the importance of the "Great Tradition" to the Chinese people today and on the political and cultural forces that have unified China despite the great variety of its regions and its peoples.

Unit 1: History

Video: "Remembering"

Readings

Introduction to Part 1, by Rhoads Murphey

1. "The Old Order," by John K. Fairbank
2. "Sung Society: Change within Tradition," by E. A. Kracke, Jr.
3. "Traditional China at Its Peak: Achievements and Problems," by John K. Fairbank
4. "China's Response to the West," edited by Ssu-yu Teng and John K. Fairbank

5. "Modern China in Transition, 1900–1950," by Mary C. Wright

Learning Objectives

To become acquainted with:

— a general outline of Chinese history

— Confucian ideology and its influence on Chinese culture and political and social institutions

— the transformation of traditional society and political institutions in the modern era

— Mao Zedong's role in modern Chinese politics

— the "Great Tradition" and the strength of historical consciousness in modern China

Overview

Chinese civilization has survived for over 4,000 years, and no summary of Chinese history can adequately do justice to its richness and complexity. Nevertheless, Rhoads Murphey's Introduction provides a succinct outline of the Chinese past. The imperial system based on Confucian principles was established during the Eastern Han dynasty (206 B.C.–220 A.D.), and it remained the basis of Chinese government until the Republican Revolution of 1911. Although China experienced periods of disorder and foreign domination, the imperial tradition and Chinese culture remained intact. For centuries Chinese culture dominated East Asia and influenced the cultures and political institutions of neighboring countries. As Murphey points out, the Chinese are very "past conscious" and their history is a source of great pride.

As John Fairbank explains in "The Old Order," the ancient principles of Confucian government, which have been explicitly repudiated since 1949, are central to an understanding of China's history. In contemporary China, even though the principles of Marxism, Leninism, and Mao Zedong Thought have supplanted Confucianism, such notions as the belief in the perfectibility of individuals are evident in the modern emphasis on political education. The Confucian concept of the individual as perfectible and having an innate moral sense influenced the Confucian philosophy of government and, together with even older Chinese understandings of the relationship between humans and nature and the concept of rule by the "Mandate of Heaven," has influenced Chinese society, culture, and political organization. The values of Confucian ideology were embodied by the scholar-gentry class, which was the main source of government officials and hence instrumental in preserving the imperial system. Fairbank also illuminates very basic Chinese attitudes toward the role of the ruler in maintaining harmony between humankind and the rest of nature, government by moral example, hierarchical social order, centralized government, and the place of the individual in society. (Note that many of these attitudes are very different from those held by most Westerners.) These topics are discussed further in subsequent sections of the *Study Guide,* as they are relevant to various aspects of Chinese tradition.

E. A. Kracke's article examines the Song (Sung) dynasty, a period many historians consider an important turning point in Chinese history. Yet, as Kracke notes, it was a period of "change within tradition." The Song dynasty witnessed a shift in population from northern China to the agriculturally rich south. This shift in population stimulated an expansion of commerce and with it a burgeoning merchant class. The growth of urban areas and of a system of currency and credit also reached unprecedented levels, though China remained primarily an agrarian society. The imperial examination system became the predominant method for bureaucratic recruitment, and many of the new recruits were from urban areas, probably from families who had acquired their wealth from commerce. Prior to the Song, many officials came from aristocratic families whose wealth was based in landholding. Expanding the scope of bureaucratic recruitment also meant greater power for the emperor, since these new recruits owed their status solely to having passed the imperial examinations. Thus, as Kracke shows, although the foundations of the Chinese polity remained the same, significant changes occurred within the traditional order. Published in 1955, this essay is also important because it anticipated a trend among Western historians away from the notion of traditional China as a changeless society.

John K. Fairbank's second article in this section, "Traditional China at Its Peak," draws on the growing literature on social and economic history that has appeared over the past decade to revise many long-standing assumptions regarding late imperial China. Recent research has revealed that the branding of traditional China as stagnant and changeless was a superficial judgment at best. Fairbank contrasts the institutional structure, which exhibited little capacity for change, with the people and economy, which experienced "rapid and tremendous growth." Fairbank presents a wide array of qualitative evidence to illustrate the extensive commercialization and regional specialization of China's economy on the eve of its clash with the militant commercial powers of the West. According to Fairbank, the vibrancy of China's economy puts the "Western 'opening' of China in a new light" and belies the importance of the "long-assumed 'Western impact.'" Yet despite an impressive level of preindustrial economic development, China's economy was mired in what some have called a "high-level equilibrium trap." Fairbank describes this situation as a "labor-intensive circular-flow economy" that inhibited industrial development. He skillfully presents a balanced portrait of China on the eve of its modern transformation.

As the video "Remembering" graphically reveals, the Chinese concept of a hierarchical society and polity, which placed the emperor, as the "son of heaven," at the pinnacle of power, was physically represented in the carefully crafted architecture of the Forbidden City. This concept of the unique status of the emperor and the Chinese empire was also extended to foreign relations. Prior to the nineteenth century, countries seeking diplomatic and commercial ties with China were required to accept the Chinese notion that they were tributary states of the Chinese empire. The documents translated by Fairbank and Ssu-yu Teng reveal the application of these Chinese attitudes toward the early intrusion of militant Western commercial powers and the growing perception of the threat these powers posed to China. The memorial of the Qianlong emperor to King George III of England displays the patronizing tone of the Chinese toward foreigners, all of whom were generally referred to as barbarians. After China's defeat by the British in the Opium Wars of the mid-nineteenth century, some Chinese officials began to recognize the need to study Western military technology, while continuing to assert the superiority of Chinese culture. But, after suffering repeated defeats at the hands of the Western powers, many Chinese began to question the efficacy of their culture or to seek ways to preserve their cultural identity while adopting Western ideas and technology. This issue continued to resurface throughout the nineteenth and twentieth centuries. The abortive "spiritual pollution" campaign of 1983, aimed at eliminating unwanted Western cultural influences, was a more recent manifestation of this dilemma.

Mary Wright, in her essay, shows how the nationalist and anti-foreign sentiments that emerged in the nineteenth century became a potent force in the twentieth century as China faced the prospect of dismemberment at the hands of foreign imperialist powers. Outlining the epochal changes that occurred in China from 1900 to 1950, when political instability, civil war, and foreign invasion racked the country, she notes that China was struck by "equivalents of the Reformation, French Revolution, and Russian Revolution." In the countryside the peasantry suffered from the dual threat of higher taxes and declining income. The success of the Communist Party resulted from the Communists' ability to mobilize the peasantry under the banners of nationalism and social reform. In urban China, Chinese entrepreneurs who had experienced success during World War I, when foreign competition abated, suffered at the hands of a predatory government and foreign competitors who enjoyed special privileges. This period also witnessed the spread of popular education and political awareness. Socialism, liberalism, anarchism, and communism all found adherents in China. Military power became an important component in politics, and ultimately the survival of the major contenders for political power, the Guomindang (Kuomintang) and the Communist Party, was due in part to their command of potent military forces.

The video "Remembering" focuses on the importance of the imperial institution in Chinese history and its role in maintaining the continuity of Chinese culture. From 221 B.C., when the emperor Qin Shihuangdi forcibly united the feudal states of ancient China, until the fall of the Qing (Ch'ing) dynasty in 1911, the centralized Chinese state remained consistent in form. Yet despite the fact that China was a centralized bureaucratic state in which the emperor wielded absolute power, there were also de facto limits on imperial power that are not evident in the video. Prior to the Song dynasty, the government was staffed by large landholders who traced their origins to the aristocratic families of feudal China. Political alliances among these families often served to check imperial power. During the Tang dynasty (618–906), the power of local military governors challenged imperial authority. During the Ming dynasty (1368–1644), imperial power was further concentrated in the hands of the emperor, but the burdens of governing led to a reliance on palace eunuchs capable of manipulating the emperor. Similarly, bureaucratic inertia often thwarted imperial initiatives. Still, the underlying trend in Chinese history was toward greater concentration of power in the hands of the emperor.

In assessing the political legacy of Mao Zedong, the video raises many complex questions. The devastating effects of the Great Leap Forward, the excesses of the Cultural Revolution, and the near deification of Mao have led some observers to cast Mao as a latter-day emperor whose arbitrary use of power and pursuit of failed policies plunged China into chaos. He is compared in particular to Qin Shihuangdi, whose unification of China was achieved at a terrible human cost. Mao's antipathy toward intellectuals is also compared to that of Qin. While it may be possible to compare Mao to a traditional emperor in terms of his use of political power, the student should think carefully about whether the analogy is valid in terms of goals and political rationale. It should be considered—as Murphey points out in his Introduction and as will become even more apparent in Part 2 of this course—that Mao's own thinking and policies changed over the nearly twenty years he was in power. His political thought was based on Marxist-Leninist doctrines; he saw his task as the transformation of a traditional agrarian society along socialist lines, while resisting both the external threat of militant imperialists and the internal threat of opponents to revolutionary change. His early success as a revolutionary leader was based on his ability to adapt Marxist-Leninist doctrines to Chinese circumstances. He turned on the intellectuals only when he saw them as an obstacle to achieving his vision of socialism. In the end he attacked all aspects of traditional culture; Mao sought to reorganize society and remold the national consciousness. No Chinese emperor ever undertook so daunting a task, and no Chinese emperor ever sought to attack the very foundations of the society and the polity. As Murphey concludes, China continues to pay a price for the failures that began with the Great Leap Forward, but "much constructive work was done; the revolution was far from being all bad."

Key Concepts

The "Great Tradition." The Great Tradition generally refers to China's aristocratic tradition, which was transmitted through Confucianism. It is often contrasted with the "Small Tradition," a combination of Daoism, Buddhism, and popular religious beliefs, as they were practiced by the common people.

Dynasty. A dynasty took its name from a sequence of rulers from the same patrilineal family. For over 2,000 years China was ruled by a series of dynasties.

Mandate of Heaven. The concept of the mandate of heaven can be traced to the early Zhou period (1027–770 B.C.). The rulers of the Zhou claimed that Heaven had given them a mandate to destroy the wicked Shang ruler and to supplant his dynasty. The Chinese believed that the virtue of an emperor was the ethical sanction for maintaining his rule. Bad conduct on the emperor's part removed the sanction and justified rebellion.

Li. The Confucian concept *li* literally means rites, but it included all those traditional forms that provided an objective standard of conduct. It has the general meaning of decorum or moral behavior according to status.

Legalism. The doctrine of Legalism, which supplied the political rationale of the Qin dynasty (221–207 B.C.), stressed the rational organization of society and resources to strengthen the state. It also held that human nature was evil and that exhaustive laws and severe punishments were necessary to expand state power and to keep people submissive and disciplined.

Scholar-gentry. Many Western sinologists have adopted the term scholar-gentry to describe the elite intelligentsia who were the primary source of government officials in traditional China. This term reflects the fact that the power of this group was based on a combination of their educational attainments and their economic power as landholders.

High-Level Equilibrium Trap. This term has been used to describe the dilemma of China's economy prior to the Opium War. Relying on a high level of premodern technology, China's economy was sufficiently productive to sustain a growing population; but the burgeoning population obviated the need for machinery or other labor-saving technology and left very little surplus for investment. What Fairbank refers to as a "circular-flow of production and consumption" prevented the creation of credit or accumulation of capital necessary for investment. While many historians have accepted this characterization of the Chinese economy, it has not gone uncriticized. For example, some historians have argued that a surplus existed, but Chinese elites squandered it on luxuries and other unproductive uses.

Century of Humiliation. The Chinese sometimes refer to the years from 1842 to 1949 as the Century of Humiliation. Beginning with the Opium War in 1842, foreign imperialist powers used military force, or the threat of force, to expand the areas of China open to foreign trade and missionary work. In the process China was compelled to accept a series of treaties that granted unequal economic and judicial rights to foreigners residing in China.

Republican Revolution of 1911. Prior to 1911 a variety of political factions loosely united under the "Revolutionary Alliance" (Tongmenghui) sought to overthrow the Qing dynasty (1644–1911). In 1911 government troops in Wuhan revolted and seized control of the city. This precipitated the defection of troops in other provinces and eventually led to the abdication of the emperor and the establishment of the republic in 1912.

May Fourth Movement. On 4 May 1919 Chinese students in Beijing held major demonstrations to protest the government's acceptance of provisions in the Versailles Treaty granting Germany's former concessions in Shandong province to Japan. The movement quickly spread throughout China's major cities, involving merchants, workers, and intellectuals. The resulting boycott of foreign goods has been acclaimed as the first nationwide expression of Chinese nationalism.

Guomindang (Kuomintang). Following the 1911 Revolution, the "Revolutionary Alliance" (Tongmenghui) was reorganized to form the Guomindang, or Nationalist Party. Originally it was a loosely organized political party representing a variety of viewpoints, though largely following the leadership of Sun Yat-sen. During the early 1920s, when the Guomindang formed a temporary united front with the Chinese Communists, the party was reorganized along strict Leninist lines. Under Guomindang leadership, China was formally unified in 1927. Also in 1927, the Guomindang and the Communists split and remained open adversaries until 1936, when they formed an uneasy alliance against the Japanese that lasted until the end of World War II. After the war open hostilities broke out; following the Communist victory in 1949, the Guomindang leadership moved to Taiwan, where it continues to dominate politics today.

Great Leap Forward. Dissatisfied with the lack of progress in the socialist transformation of Chinese society, in 1958 Mao Zedong launched an ambitious campaign known as the Great Leap Forward. The Great Leap Forward stressed mass mobilization, political education, and self-reliance and was designed to increase agricultural and industrial productivity while simultaneously reorganizing society. Poor planning, the withdrawal of economic aid from the Soviet Union, and bad weather doomed the Great Leap Forward to failure and led to severe famine in some regions of China.

Cultural Revolution. The Cultural Revolution was a major sociopolitical upheaval that affected all aspects of life in China for nearly a decade. Mao Zedong launched the Cultural Revolution in 1966 as a means to realize his own vision of socialist modernization. The Cultural Revolution began as a debate in literary circles, but it soon evolved into a criticism of all remnants of Chinese tradition. It became a mass movement led by Chinese youth who took the writings of Mao as their guide. Individuals, especially intellectuals, were physically attacked and were sent to the countryside to learn from the peasants. Eventually the army had to be called in to restore order. The movement was also a political struggle employed by Mao to eliminate from power many of his political rivals. During the Cultural Revolution, Party and government administration was reorganized to include more workers and peasants in an effort to blunt the influence of intellectuals and to overturn the status quo, which Mao felt was inhibiting the development of socialism in China. During this period, most major universities and schools were closed, and, consequently, an entire generation of Chinese youth never received a proper education. The present leadership, many of whom were victims of the Cultural Revolution, have repudiated the movement and now refer to it as the "ten years of disorder."

Review Questions

1. What was the state of Chinese civilization in 2000 B.C., according to Murphey's Introduction?

2. What is the origin of our word "China," and why is it an appropriate term, according to Murphey?

3. As discussed in the Fairbank article, "The Old Order," what are: (a) the Chinese view of the human relationship to nature? (b) the "Mandate of Heaven" and its political applications? (c) the Confucian understanding of human nature? How do these find expression in the Confucian ideal of "good government"?

4. What factors spurred the development of the Chinese bureaucracy, and what were its essential administrative principles, according to Fairbank?

5. According to Kracke, what factors caused the population shift during the Song period, and what were the economic and social consequences?

6. What impact did the expansion of cities have on Chinese culture in the Song period?

7. In what ways does Fairbank's article, "Traditional China at Its Peak," represent a departure from previous interpretations of late Imperial

China? What does Fairbank mean when he describes China as having achieved a high degree of "homeostasis" by 1800?

8. What does Fairbank identify as important economic and social developments in China prior to 1800? What reason does Fairbank offer to explain the "non-emergence of capitalism" in the Chinese economy?

9. As reflected in the documents on China's response to the West, what were the changing attitudes of the Chinese toward foreigners in the nineteenth century?

10. What are the roots of Chinese nationalism, as discussed by Wright, and what was the role of nationalism in the eventual victory of the Communist revolution?

11. What are some of the misconceptions about China often held by Westerners, according to Wright?

12. What was the Cultural Revolution—its aims, methods, and effects?

13. According to the video "Remembering," what are the symbolic meanings of the Forbidden City and the Great Wall?

Unit 2: Geographic and Ethnic Diversity

Video: "Eating"

Readings

Introduction to Part 1, by Rhoads Murphey

6. "The Chinese Scene," by John K. Fairbank
7. "Man and Nature in China," by Rhoads Murphey
8. "Patterns of Nature and Man," by R. R. C. de Crespigny
9. "Regional Urbanization in Nineteenth-Century China," by G. William Skinner
10. "City as a Mirror of Society," by Rhoads Murphey

Learning Objectives

To become acquainted with:

— the major physiographic regions of China

— the geographic and ethnic diversity of China

— Chinese attitudes toward nature and the individual

— patterns of urbanization and regional development

— the insecurity of the food supply, the preoccupation with food, and the ritual quality of eating

Overview

The Chinese have maintained a remarkable degree of political and cultural unity in historical and contemporary times despite enormous geographic and ethnic diversity. The articles by Fairbank and de Crespigny provide a neat summary of these variations, particularly the contrast between north and south. The Yangzi river serves as a dividing line between the arid plains of northern China and the lush river valleys of the south. As we see in the video "Eating," environmental factors have shaped the lifestyles of the Chinese people. The need to feed a large population has conditioned the form and intensity of Chinese agriculture. There is less than one-half acre of food-producing soil per person and little room for expansion. Thus, the emphasis is on grain production, with only a minimal amount of land given over to animal husbandry. Chinese agriculture is very labor intensive. The high yields of the rice-producing regions of southern China require huge inputs of human labor. Because the task of transplanting rice seedlings is so delicate, suitable mechanization has not yet been developed. The social costs of mechanization would also be great, since there would be few outlets for the surplus labor that mechanization would create. De Crespigny echoes many of Fairbank's points while providing a more technical description of the mountain ranges and rivers of China.

Centuries of intensive agriculture have altered the physiographic features of China but, as Rhoads Murphey notes in "Man and Nature in China," the Chinese approach to nature differs markedly from that of

Western nations. The Chinese conceive of human beings as part of a grander natural order, and agricultural practices are designed to maximize the use of natural processes. The natural environment has been altered to supply humans with sustenance, but this has been done in cooperation with nature. This respect for nature is evident in Chinese art and literature, which portray nature in a reverent context. The rewards in high yields and bountiful harvests accruing to the traditional Chinese agriculturists' harmonious utilization of natural resources no doubt reinforced this cooperative approach to nature. Murphey goes on to note that in modern China nature has been "dethroned" and a confident, pioneering, creative communist individual put in its place. The mobilization of labor has had both economic and political objectives. Economically, the Chinese continue to achieve greater yields from existing resources. Politically, the Communist Party uses mass mobilization to instill political values.

G. William Skinner is an anthropologist whose regional analysis of Chinese urbanization has had a great influence on Western studies of Chinese society, polity, and economy. Relating historical development to geography, Skinner defines nine physiographic regions in China within which discrete urban networks were formed. Within these regions resources of all kinds—social, cultural, economic, and political—were utilized and exploited. By dividing China into these nine macroregions, Skinner supplies a useful tool of analysis which helps explain the variation in historical cycles of regional development.

While Skinner's article explains the urbanization process in nineteenth-century China, Rhoads Murphey's second article discusses urbanization as a reflection of Chinese cultural values in both imperial and contemporary times. Cities were primarily centers of imperial authority, and as such were symbols of Confucian virtues of order and designed to project imperial power into the countryside. The county *(xian)* capitals were carefully laid out in a precise geometric fashion. Imposed on a varied landscape, county capitals were designed to control and tax the countryside, the source of wealth in an agrarian society. Unlike Western cities, they did not serve as political centers that could potentially challenge imperial authority. Similarly, there was no contempt on the part of city dwellers for rural people, who were held in high esteem. Many Chinese elites were themselves natives of the countryside and kept close ties with their native villages.

Chinese civilization has survived in part because of the enormous resourcefulness and hard work of Chinese farmers. The monumental irrigation works and the terracing of mountainsides are striking examples of how the Chinese have altered their environment. When nature cannot be harnessed to serve man, technology must be developed to make the best of limited resources. The Chinese cooking pan, the wok, and the practice of carefully slicing ingredients before cooking are designed to minimize the amount of fuel used to prepare food. Also significant is the Chinese attitude toward food, which as the video clearly illustrates, has a ritualized quality that stems from a memory of past periods of scarcity and famine.

The video "Eating" reveals the geographic diversity and regional specialties of Chinese cuisine, as well as the ongoing struggle to feed an ever-growing population. Beginning in southern China, where culinary arts are most highly developed, we see the art of Chinese cooking at its best. Many foreigners find Chinese food exotic, but even the Chinese themselves are awed by the strangeness of some Cantonese dishes. Economic reforms have allowed for the establishment of small-scale private enterprises, and some the most successful have been the family-run restaurants, such as that of the chicken-seller shown in the video. Still, as the narrator remarks, the elaborate feasting pictured in the video is not the norm. Banquets are special occasions, and the typical Chinese family continues to subsist on more simple fare, like the meal of the Muslim family of north China shown in the video. Despite the penchant for elaborate feasting, the burdens of a vast population and the intensity of Chinese agriculture limit the degree to which the Chinese can indulge themselves.

Key Concepts

China Proper. The term "China Proper" generally refers to those provinces of China that historically formed the core of the Chinese empire. They include the present-day provinces of Hebei, Henan, Shaanxi, Shanxi, Gansu, Shandong, Hubei, Hunan, Jiangsu, Zhejiang,

Fujian, Taiwan, Guangdong, Guangxi, Yunnan, Guizhou, Sichuan, Anhui, and Jiangxi.

Outer Areas. Tibet, Xinjiang, Mongolia, and Manchuria are sometimes referred to as outer areas. Each of these regions contains large populations of ethnic minorities. Historically they were not always incorporated into the Chinese empire.

Autonomous Regions. Very soon after the establishment of the People's Republic of China, autonomous administrative units were organized at all levels of administration in areas inhabited by minority nationalities. National autonomous areas include autonomous regions, autonomous prefectures, autonomous *xian* (counties), and autonomous banners. First-order autonomous regions are the largest and include the Inner Mongolian Autonomous Region, the Xinjiang Uighur Autonomous Region, the Guangxi Zhuang Autonomous Region, the Ningxia Hui Autonomous Region, and the Tibetan Autonomous Region. All autonomous regions, regardless of size, are completely integrated into the regular centralized administrative hierarchy. They have neither more nor less authority than regular administrative units and differ only in that concessions are made to local minority customs and language and that a special effort is made to integrate minority cadres into the administrative structure.

Review Questions

1. According to Murphey's Introduction, what is the distinction between "China Proper" and the outer areas, and what have been the relations between them?

2. What are the major regional contrasts in China, as discussed by Murphey in the Introduction and by Fairbank in chapter 6? What are the basic geographic and climatic influences?

3. According to Fairbank, how has the physical environment of China shaped the "distinctly Chinese way of life"?

4. What is the difference between the traditional Chinese attitude toward nature and the attitude since the revolution of 1949, as discussed

by Murphey in "Man and Nature in China"? How do these attitudes compare with those in the West?

5. What are the reasons for the revolutionary change in attitude toward the natural world in the People's Republic? What are some of the benefits and risks of the new attitude, as described by Murphey?

6. As presented by de Crespigny, what are the major topographical features of China? What are China's major crops and industrial resources?

7. Why does Skinner use a regional approach to understanding urbanization in nineteenth-century China?

8. What does Skinner define as the determining factors for the location of regional "cores"?

9. What were the the actual and symbolic roles of China's cities in imperial times, as discussed by Murphey in "City as a Mirror of Society"? How did they mirror the values of imperial China? How do China's modern cities reflect contemporary goals and values?

10. According to Murphey, what was the traditionally perceived relationship between city and countryside in China? What have been the attitudes toward cities under different Communist leaders?

11. What is the Chinese attitude toward food? Why has food always been such a preoccupation? What have been the major problems of food production, and how have the Chinese dealt with them?

Essay/Discussion Questions for Part 1

1. What factors have contributed to China's political and cultural unity?

Suggested guidelines:

a. Consider the Confucian tradition, referring especially to:

- Murphey's Introduction

• "The Old Order" and "The Chinese Scene" by Fairbank and the role of Confucian ideology and Chinese attitudes toward nature and the individual

b. Examine the imperial tradition, with reference to:

• the examination of the historical background and evaluation of the strengths of the imperial tradition in the video "Remembering"

• the video "Remembering," Fairbank's treatment in the text of the "Mandate of Heaven" concept, the role of the emperor, and the nature of the bureaucratic order that stemmed from "imperial Confucianism"

• Murphey's Introduction on the achievements of the Qin (Ch'in) and Han dynasties, and the historical and continuing role of a strong, centralized government

• Kracke's article on the precedent for "change within tradition"

c. Consider historical consciousness in China, referring to:

• Murphey's Introduction, the video "Remembering," and the documents about China's response to the West concerning Chinese pride in the imperial ideal and Chinese civilization

• the Wright article and the video "Remembering," concerning the significance of nationalism

d. Consider the importance of language, as discussed in Murphey's Introduction.

2. What geographic and political factors have exerted pressures against the maintenance of a unitary Chinese state?

Suggested guidelines:

a. Review China's geography, referring to:

• Murphey's Introduction and the selections by Fairbank and de Crespigny concerning major regional contrasts and physical barriers between some regions

• the effect of regional differences on lifestyles and cultures, as depicted in the video "Eating"

• Murphey's discussion, in his Introduction, of the ethnic and cultural variations in China and the distinction between China Proper and the Outer Areas

• Skinner's discussion of regionalism and de Crespigny's account of the geographic factors effecting changes in political power bases

b. Consider the political factors that have encouraged disunity, referring to:

• Murphey's Introduction, concerning the history and political styles of different dynasties; rebellions; foreign pressure, invasion, rule, and "spheres of influence"; and differing attitudes toward reform held by the Nationalists and the Communists

• de Crespigny's view of the constraints on modernization

• the divisions caused among the people by changing attitudes toward nature and modernization, as outlined by Murphey in "Man and Nature"

• Murphey's discussion, in "City as a Mirror of Society," of the traditional relationship between urban and rural areas, and the changes since 1949

Part 2

Politics

Part 2 introduces a political tradition that is more than 2,000 years old. This section of the course discusses the political systems of both traditional and contemporary China, examining political thought, national political institutions, and the interaction between the political system and the individual.

Unit 3: Ideology and Organization

Video: "Believing"

Readings

Introduction to Part 2, by Steven M. Goldstein

11. "Sources of Chinese Tradition," Confucius / Mencius / Han Fei
12. "The Political Tradition," by John K. Fairbank
13. "The Chinese Revolution," by Mao Zedong
14. "Ideology after Mao," CCP Constitution / Deng Xiaoping / Zhao Ziyang / Li Peng
15. "China after Mao," by Steven M. Goldstein, Kathrin Sears, and Richard C. Bush
16. "Institutionalizing the Post-Mao Reforms," by Harry Harding

17. "The Origins of China's Pro-Democracy Movement," by Yasheng Huang

Learning Objectives

To become acquainted with:

— the principal tenets of traditional Chinese religious and ethical beliefs

— the Confucian and Legalist political tradition

— the structure of political organization in modern China and its historical antecedents

— some basic principles of Mao Zedong Thought

— political developments in China since the death of Mao Zedong

— the challenges posed to Communist ideology by new efforts to improve material well-being

Overview

Some aspects of the Chinese political system have already been touched on in the video "Remembering" and in Part 1, but this unit of the course examines more systematically the political thought and organization of China. Since the establishment of the People's Republic of China in 1949, Marxism-Leninism and Mao Zedong Thought together have been the official ideology of China. Unit 3 and the video "Believing" investigate both the recent challenges to the current political orthodoxy and the political and religious beliefs of the past, which continue to influence political thought in China.

Three major branches of thought—Confucianism, which expounded a code of moral conduct; Daoism, a uniquely Chinese religion emphasizing harmony with nature; and Buddhism, which offers a path to salvation and the promise of an afterlife—have all coexisted for centuries and continue to influence Chinese culture. The durability of these three diverse belief systems and their continued influence on Chinese thought are testimony to the practical and eclectic approach to religion that the Chinese have evinced throughout their history. Also important are the numerous popular religious beliefs, frequently based on local superstitions or legends. These popular beliefs provided solace to the masses and in times of political turmoil served to unify peasant rebellions.

Confucianism was the official political ideology of China from the Han dynasty (206 B.C.–220 A.D.) until the Revolution of 1911. While Confucianism underwent various interpretations over the centuries, fundamental principles, such as leadership by moral example and the belief in the innate goodness and perfectibility of human beings, remained constant. Prior to the Han dynasty the doctrine of Legalism, which was favored by Qin Shihuangdi, the first unifier of China, was a potent competitor to Confucianism. Legalism placed little faith in human nature and advocated strict laws as a means of controlling human behavior. The excerpts in "Sources of Chinese Tradition" highlight the major differences between these two schools of thought. Although Confucianism eventually triumphed, elements of Legalism were incorporated into it to strengthen the structure of bureaucratic rule.

The formal and informal components of political organization in traditional China are outlined in John Fairbank's article. As he notes, although the emperor retained absolute power, the government was administered by a centralized bureaucracy. The formal governmental structure was carefully delineated, with forms of communication, terms of office, and administrative rankings all rigidly defined. At the national level, government administration was in the hands of the Six Boards and, in descending order, provincial governors and county magistrates. Beneath the county level, formal administration was virtually nonexistent, and local problems were often handled by resident members of the scholar-gentry, whose prestige was based on a combination of economic power and educational attainment. According to Fairbank, the imperial government "rested upon the gentry as its foundation" and never directly penetrated the villages.

Mao Zedong assumed the leadership of the Chinese Communist Party during the 1930s, and his political thought remains an integral component of official Chinese ideology. The text contains some excerpts from Mao's writings that illustrate both the consistency and flexibility of Mao's thought. In the first excerpt Mao explains the policy of New Democracy, which was intended to be a prefatory stage for the development of socialism. It is very important to consider New Democracy in its historical context. In 1947 the Communist Party was still engaged in a civil war with the Guomindang government, and support from non-Communist elements was considered essential to the success of the revolution. Thus, Mao defined the enemies of the revolution in very narrow terms: the feudal landlord class and monopoly capitalists. Middle peasants and the national bourgeoisie were assured of a place in the political order, but the supremacy of the Communist Party, the leadership of the proletariat and the peasants, and the eventual goal of socialism were also clearly stated. The second and third excerpts were written during the late 1950s, after the Communist Party had consolidated its power. These writings reflect Mao's dissatisfaction with the pace of the socialist transformation of Chinese society and his disenchantment with the Soviet model of development. Thus, Mao espoused a theory of "permanent revolution," criticizing the the blind copying of the Soviet Union and urging a rapid and continual advance toward socialism. Mao's goal, a socialist society, remained consistent, but his strategy for achieving this goal had changed. Similarly, the present regime has rejected many of Mao's strategies, but, as stated in the Constitution of 1982, Mao's thought remains a key component of Chinese ideology.

Goldstein, Sears, and Bush describe the current political organization of the People's Republic of China. This structure follows the Soviet model, with the Communist Party hierarchy mirroring governmental organization. Most major decisions are made in executive committees according to Marxist-Leninist principles of democratic centralism. Representative bodies exist, but their function is to ratify decisions of the executive committees. Policy is implemented through the bureaucracy, which at times has proved unresponsive or obstructionist. The age-old problems of the bureaucratic state—nepotism, corruption, and bureaucratic footdragging—persist and, some say, were exacerbated by the sudden policy shifts that characterized the Cultural Revolution.

The new Constitution of the Communist Party of 1982 marked the official retreat from the ideological fervor of the Maoist era and placed a renewed emphasis on improving material well-being. Achieving its goal of economic modernization also required political reforms. Harry Harding, a highly respected authority on contemporary Chinese politics, explores the goals and ramifications of the political reforms in his essay. According to Harding, the reforms were meant to raise the level of education and technical expertise of Communist Party members, while reducing the Party's direct control over the government bureaucracy and state-run enterprises. These political reforms were necessary to prepare the Party to implement the ambitious economic reforms designed to bring about the modernization of China's economy by the year 2000.

In the eyes of some Party members, the emphasis on economic modernization and improving living standards poses a threat to the ideological foundations of socialist society. Many Communist leaders lament the apparent materialism that seems to have taken hold of China's younger generation. By 1987 criticism of economic reform on ideological grounds had become more widespread. In response to such criticism, Zhao Ziyang's speech of October 1987, excerpted in the reader, defended the reforms and urged their continued expansion. A firm supporter of economic reform, Zhao issued an appeal to nationalism by stressing the uniqueness of China's situation, combined with a careful effort to explain economic reform in terms of Marxist thought by asserting that China was in a primary stage of socialism.

The need to balance practical and material consideration with ideological concerns was a major challenge to Chinese reformers. By 1986 China's Communist leadership also faced popular protests. In December of 1986, Chinese students at several major universities demonstrated in favor of more democratic government. In this case, the government responded swiftly, but peacefully, to halt the demonstrations. Several prominent dissidents were expelled from the Party, and the government launched an ideological counter-offensive against "bourgeois liberalization." Although the reaction was restrained, excerpts from a speech that Deng Xiaoping delivered in December 1986 indicate that Party leaders took these protests quite seriously. Although Deng advocated the use of persuasion, he ominously warned that if the demonstrators disturb order or violate the law, "they must be dealt with unhesitatingly."

In April of 1989, the death of Hu Yaobang, who was ousted as head of the Party as a result of the demonstrations of 1986, occasioned renewed protests by students, which gradually gained broad popular support in Beijing and other cities. After nearly two months of protest, Deng unleashed the army, and in June of 1989 the world witnessed the bloody suppression of prodemocracy demonstrators in Tiananmen Square. In the aftermath, the Chinese premier, Li Peng, emerged as a major spokesman for more conservative elements in the leadership and replaced Zhao Ziyang as head of the Communist Party. The reader includes an excerpt from a speech in which Li attempted to explain the prodemocracy movement as a conspiracy to subvert socialism. Li attributed the unrest to a "handful of people" who took advantage of the students. Li maintained that economic development could not proceed without political stability and called for a renewed program of ideological and political work.

Many analysts have attributed the 1989 demonstrations to the gap between political and economic reforms. Citing the flaws in both the economic and political reforms, Yasheng Huang offers a somewhat different interpretation of the prodemocracy movement. As Huang points out, there was widespread resentment at the corruption and "rampant inflation," two unwelcomed side-effects of poorly implemented economic reforms. Similarly, political reforms also entailed a high cost. For example, in an effort to induce antireform elements in the leadership to retire, outgoing leaders were able to garner promotions for their relatives and friends to key positions. According to Huang, this blatant cronyism and nepotism tarnished the Party's reputation and compromised the efforts of reformist leaders to reorganize the Party. The failure to institutionalize the political process was readily apparent in the example of Deng Xiaoping, who relinquished all formal positions in the Party and government, but remained the "de facto supreme leader." In so doing, Deng undercut the authority of the formal organs of the government and Party. Huang concludes that the economic reforms represent an "inherently unstable halfway house" between a planned and market economy, while political reform was a temporary expedient that did nothing to undo the personalization of the political process.

Key Concepts

Li. See Unit 1.

Legalism. See Unit 1.

The Five Relationships. The Five Relationships and their appropriate forms are affection between parent and child; righteousness between ruler and subject; distinction between husband and wife; order between old and young; and sincerity between friends. The Five Relationships constitute the central values of Confucian society.

Daoism (Taoism). In its original form Daoism was a philosophical system deriving chiefly from the *Daodejing (Tao Te Ching),* a book traditionally ascribed to Laozi. It describes the individual's ideal state as freedom from desire and a life of effortless simplicity, achieved by following the Dao (the Way), the spontaneous creative functioning of the universe. Quietistic in nature, Daoists condemned the social virtues expounded by Confucius. Later Daoism stressed the search for immortality, supposed to flow from the Dao, and also encouraged the practice of alchemy. By the fifth century A.D., Daoism had incorporated many elements of Mahayana Buddhism and offered a more developed religious system.

The New Democratic Revolution. Mao devised the theory of the New Democratic Revolution during the Sino-Japanese War. According to this theory, the Communist Party would assume the leadership of a broad united front of all revolutionary elements: workers, peasants, and segments of the middle class. The purpose of the New Democratic Revolution was the defeat of foreign aggressors and the overthrow of reactionary elements at home. The New Democratic Revolution emphasized anti-imperialism, honest government, and socioeconomic reform while downplaying class struggle. This policy was designed to garner broad support during the later stages of the revolution and the early years of the People's Republic of China, but Mao always maintained that the New Democratic Revolution was merely a preparatory stage that would eventually give way to a socialist revolution, which could only be accomplished under the leadership of the Communist Party.

Permanent Revolution. In the late 1950s Mao became increasingly concerned that the emphasis on economic growth was leading to a degeneration of revolutionary values, complacency among Chinese bureaucrats, and the reemergence of class enemies in society. Thus, despite the establishment of a socialist society, contradictions continued to exist. Mao's response was the theory of "permanent revolution," which emphasized the mobilization and politicization of the masses, struggle against intellectuals and technical specialists, and a general emphasis on revolutionary egalitarianism. These policies were hallmarks of the Great Leap Forward and the Cultural Revolution.

Constitution of 1982. The Constitution of 1982, written under the guidance of Deng Xiaoping and his reformist supporters, represents a rejection of the more radical policies of the Maoist era. It criticizes the emphasis on class struggle and distrust of intellectuals and stresses economic growth and improved standards of living. Excerpts from the preamble of the Constitution of 1982 are reprinted in chapter 14.

Four Cardinal Principles. In the post-Mao reform era the Chinese Communist Party defined four inviolable principles that were to be upheld through the reform period. These were adherence to socialism, adherence to the people's democratic dictatorship, leadership of the Communist Party, and adherence to Marxism-Leninism and Mao Zedong Thought.

Dual System of Party and State. In China, as in other Communist countries, the Communist Party organization parallels the formal government apparatus. Most major political decisions are made within Party organs, but these decisions are implemented through the state apparatus under the supervision of the Party.

Cadre. In every major political, economic, and cultural unit in China there are cadres, Communist Party members responsible for organizing the unit and implementing Party politics.

The Four Modernizations. The Four Modernizations is the policy to modernize agriculture, industry, science and technology, and national defense by the year 2000. It was proposed by Zhou Enlai in January 1975.

Review Questions

1. What were the factors involved in the decay of China's traditional system of government, according to Goldstein's Introduction?

2. What adaptations did Mao make in Marxist-Leninist theory, according to Goldstein?

3. What are the main differences in political philosophy between the Confucians and the Legalists?

4. According to Fairbank, what was the basic organization of the imperial bureaucracy, and how was centralized control maintained?

5. The Chinese gentry were an essential, but informal, pillar of imperial rule in traditional China. How is the complex role of the gentry illustrated in Fairbank's definitions of the gentry?

6. What is the difference in emphasis between Mao's 1947 speech and his later speeches, as excerpted in the text?

7. Why does Goldstein consider the Great Leap Forward of 1958–1960 a watershed in the development of the Chinese political system?

8. What is Mao Zedong's theory of permanent revolution or continuous struggle?

9. What is the principal contradiction in Chinese society, according to the preamble of the 1982 Constitution of the Communist Party?

10. As outlined by Goldstein, Sears, and Bush, what are the two parts of the Chinese political structure, and what are the organizational levels of administration?

11. What problems in the bureaucracy is the Deng government trying to correct, as discussed by Goldstein et al.?

12. What problems have been generated by the Cultural Revolution and by the new prosperity?

13. What were the ideological issues addressed in the speeches of Deng Xiaoping, Zhao Ziyang, and Li Peng? How did these leaders differ in their efforts to balance ideological concerns with the need for economic reform?

14. Contrast the economic and political reforms of the post-Mao era. How were the reforms interrelated? According to Harding, what were the three problems that the political reforms sought to remedy? According to Huang, how were China's political and economic reforms flawed from the start?

15. As presented in the video "Believing," what are the major tenets of Buddhism, Daoism, Confucianism, and popular Chinese religions? What values do traditional Chinese beliefs and Communism seem to share, according to the video?

Unit 4: The Individual and the State

Video: "Correcting"

Readings

Introduction to Part 2, by Steven M. Goldstein

18. "Two Models of Law," by Victor H. Li
19. "Law in Imperial China: Cases from the *Hsing-an Hui-lan*," with commentary by Derk Bodde and Clarence Morris
20. "Mr. Wang vs. Mr. Ch'en: A High Ch'ing Parable," by Frederic Wakeman, Jr.
21. "The One Who Loved Dog Meat," by B. Michael Frolic
22. "Liberalizing Political Life," by Harry Harding
23. "Political Participation in Communist China," by James R. Townsend

24. "China after Mao: The Emergence of Dissent," Fang Lizhi / Beijing University Handbill / Workers' Union Handbill
25. "China after Mao: Consequences of Dissent," Deng Xiaoping / Amnesty International

Learning Objectives

To become acquainted with:

— aspects of the traditional Chinese legal system

— the evolution and development of the Chinese legal system since 1949

— the present procedures of criminal prosecution and the goals and methods of the penal system

— the nature and meaning of political participation in China

— sources of popular unrest and the ongoing suppression of political dissent

Overview

In exploring the interaction between the individual and the state in China, this unit focuses on the legal system, which even in its contemporary form retains influences from past ideologies, and on the nature and extent of political participation.

Historically, the Chinese have had an ambivalent attitude toward law. As noted in the previous section, Confucianism stressed the innate goodness and perfectibility of the individual. According to Mencius, proper education would ensure that people would accept their respective roles and responsibilities in the social hierarchy and act accordingly, thereby making codified law unnecessary. Although local magistrates were available to adjudicate disputes, numerous proverbs can be cited to illustrate the popular disdain of litigation. Reflecting the limited penetration of the state into village life, private mediation was the preferred method of conflict resolution. Criminal matters could not be handled in this fashion, however, and by the Tang dynasty (618–

908), the Chinese had established a detailed law code, which became a model for many other countries in East Asia.

The hypothetical case of Mr. Wang versus Mr. Ch'en, discussed by Frederic Wakeman, illustrates one reason why the average citizen of imperial China was reluctant to resort to litigation. An individual's standing in society was often more important than the merits of the suit he or she might bring before the magistrate. Nevertheless, the administration of justice in imperial China was not entirely arbitrary. The examples presented in the reading by Bodde and Morris were precedent-setting cases taken from a Qing dynasty (1644–1911) handbook for magistrates. Once a case made its way into the official legal system, investigations were painstakingly thorough. Criminal cases were regarded as disruptions of the natural social harmony, and precise punishments were required to restore that harmony. Since cases involving homicide were automatically reviewed by higher authorities, local magistrates were very careful in their deliberations and verdicts.

Since 1949 the Chinese legal system has undergone several reforms. According to Victor Li, the Chinese legal system has alternated between an "external" and "internal" model. This dichotomy is indicative of changing political currents and also reflects the historical Chinese ambivalence toward the use of formal law. The internal model is based on a lengthy and continuing educational process in which an individual learns and internalizes socially accepted values. Resonances with Confucian tradition are readily apparent. The external model, which more closely resembles a Western-style legal system, has recently been reinstated in reaction to the abuses of the politicized people's courts of the Cultural Revolution era.

In the video "Correcting," elements of Western-style judicature are apparent in the workings of China's reformed legal system, but the emphasis on the social context of the crime, the need to reeducate the criminal, and the effects of the crime on the accused's family reflect traditional Chinese concerns. Defense attorneys do not assume the adversarial role of their Western counterparts, as is evident from the judge's impatience with the arguments of the defense attorney. By the time a case reaches trial, the only outstanding issue seems to be sentencing. Contrite offenders are more likely to receive lenient sentences, and it seems that there is little to be gained from resisting authority. As we learn from B. Michael Frolic's reading, this is true of the penal system as well. Evidence of rehabilitation is very important, and prison authorities can extend the sentences of recalcitrant offenders.

James Townsend's essay compares the Chinese Communist style of political participation with that of Western democracies. Compared to traditional China, political participation increased significantly after 1949, but political participation remains largely limited to government- and Party-sanctioned activities. While Mao dominated Chinese politics, mass mobilization was an important tool for carrying forward Party policies, but as Harry Harding points out, political life was reshaped during the early 1980s, in part to garner popular support for economic reform. Less political study, relaxation of control over the arts and entertainment, and a strengthening of the legal system were all designed to regain the trust of the people, particularly intellectuals and technicians who were abused during the Cultural Revolution. As Harding also notes, the apparent "liberalization" of political life also had strict limitations. Most importantly, the Party would not tolerate independent political parties, mass media, or professional associations.

As economic reforms went forward in the 1980s, the Communist Party increasingly staked its legitimacy on successful economic reform and improvements in living standards. Consequently, rampant inflation and corruption generated widespread dissent that threatened the Party's leadership. Some dissidents, such as the astrophysicist Fang Lizhi, spoke out eloquently and forcefully for democratization and human rights. Dissent was not limited to noted intellectuals. As the handbills from Beijing University and the Workers' Union indicate, students and workers also harbored bitter resentment at the corruption and wastefulness of China's leaders.

By the spring of 1989, Chinese students took to the streets to demonstrate for further political reform and to protest official corruption. Deng Xiaoping ordered the army to quell what he insisted was a "counterrevolutionary coup." Deng's address to the army shortly after the crackdown was most revealing. Ignoring the human cost of the suppression, Deng praised veteran cadres for their support, minimized the depth of popular discontent, and warned against Western influences, but also reasserted the correctness of the reform program. Deng criticized advocates of Western-style democracy, but seemed to dismiss the entire prodemocracy movement as a temporary detour on the road to modernization under the leadership of the Communist Party. Amnesty International's report, however, provides a more detailed account of the killing that occurred on June 4 and the ensuing repression of dissidents. One thing is certain: the events of June 4 have seriously diminished the prestige of both the Party and the army. While the suppression of dissent seems to have succeeded in the short term, the underlying causes of the protest movement have not been remedied.

Key Concepts

"Internal" and "External" Models of Law. Victor Li's article describes the development of the post-1949 system in terms of the competition between two models of law. The internal model, which resembles the Confucian concept of law, relies on moral suasion and education. The external model, resembling the Legalist approach to law, is based on formal, written legal codes.

Political Participation. The nature of political participation in China, the involvement of the ordinary citizen in the political process, is very different from our Western notion. In China participation consists of taking part in the implementation of predetermined policies. The process of political participation is meant to educate citizens in the goals and aspirations of the regime and to create a motivated citizenry that accepts the basic policies of the regime through involvement in their implementation.

Review Questions

1. What did the saying "heaven is high and the emperor is far away" imply about the relationship of most Chinese to politics?

2. Give some examples of the successes and failures of the Chinese Communists' attempts to encourage political participation.

3. What does Victor Li mean when he refers to the "internal" and the "external" models of law? What are the basic rationales and objectives of each model?

4. In the two cases illustrated in "Law in Imperial China," what evidence is there of the application of Confucian principles?

5. What options were open to Mr. Wang and Mr. Ch'en, respectively, in their legal dispute, as told in the parable by Wakeman? How does the outcome reflect the workings of the legal and political system of Qing society?

6. What was the aim of the state's imprisonment of "the one who loved dog meat," and how did this prisoner deal with the system?

7. What are the five major differences between Chinese Communist and Western democratic styles of political participation, according to Townsend?

8. What does Townsend mean by "latent" functions of some social behavior in relation to political participation?

9. In the video "Correcting," what traditional Chinese social values are still affecting the goals and methods of the legal system? What changes in legal measures have occurred since the Cultural Revolution?

10. According to Harding, what motivated the Communist Party to "liberalize" political life after the Cultural Revolution? How was liberalization limited?

11. What were some of the major issues raised by Chinese dissidents such as Fang Lizhi?

12. What do the Beijing University and Workers' Union handbills indicate were the sources of popular discontent?

13. How did Deng Xiaoping justify the violent suppression of the prodemocracy movement?

Essay/Discussion Questions for Part 2

1. In what ways are the traditional political philosophies and structure of China evident in Chinese Communist ideology and government?

Suggested guidelines:

a. Consider the nature of traditional Chinese society, referring to:

- the "Sources of Chinese Tradition" selections in the text, especially Confucian ideas of self-cultivation, social organization, and the role of government; and Legalist attitudes toward government control and law

- Fairbank's discussion of the imperial bureaucracy and its hierarchical structure, and local government, with attention to the balance between centralization and local autonomy

- the articles "Sources of Chinese Tradition" and "Law in Imperial China" particularly as they describe the balance between rule by law and rule by men

b. Review the organization of the state since 1949, with reference to:

- the Introduction by Goldstein, on political ideology in China since 1949

- Mao's speech stating his view of the power of the state in restructuring society, and the Chinese Constitution regarding the aim of a "socialist spiritual civilization"

- the video "Believing" on the attitude toward Mao during the Cultural Revolution

- Goldstein et al., on the hierarchical structure of the dual party/state system

2. How has the relationship of Chinese citizens to the state continued in traditional ways, and how has it changed since 1949?

Suggested guidelines:

a. Consider the traditional and modern legal systems, with reference to:

- the Introduction by Goldstein, on Confucian and Legalist attitudes toward law, and their past and continuing influence on Chinese law

- Victor Li's article, examining two legal models

- the two imperial law cases included in the text and the extent to which they embody Li's models

- "Mr. Wang vs. Mr. Chen" and the attitudes of the two men toward the workings of the law

- the video "Correcting" and the persistence of traditional values

- B. Michael Frolic's "The One Who Loved Dog Meat"

b. Examine the state's attitude toward popular political participation, with reference to:

- the Introduction by Goldstein, discussing traditional and modern attitudes

- Townsend's article analyzing the characteristics of China's current style of political participation

- the limitations that the Party imposes on independent political movements

- official corruption and popular discontent

- the brutal suppression of the 1989 prodemocracy demonstrations

Part 3

Society

Part 3 introduces the basic social organization of both imperial and contemporary China. This section of the course focuses on the family as the basic unit of social life, on broader forms of community that link individuals and families, and on cleavages among different elements in the complex society of China.

Unit 5: The Chinese Family

Video: "Marrying"

Readings

Introduction to Part 3, by Martin K. Whyte

26. "Family Instructions," edited by Patricia B. Ebrey

27. "The Family," by Ba Jin

28. "Urban Workers' Housework," by Wang Yalin and Li Jinrong

29. "Zhao Xiuyin: Lady of the Sties," by Mary Sheridan

30. "Courtship, Love, and Marriage: The Life and Times of Yu Luojin," by Emily Honig

Learning Objectives

To become acquainted with:

- — the importance of the family as a social and economic unit
- — the traditional rules of conduct governing Chinese families
- — the strength of traditional moral values and their continuing influence on Chinese families
- — Chinese marriage customs and rituals
- — the status of women in traditional Chinese society and changes in their status since 1949
- — contemporary Chinese attitudes toward the family, marriage, and divorce
- — the quality of life in contemporary urban China

Overview

Throughout Chinese history the family has been the most important social and economic unit. Unlike Western societies, where individualism is prized, Chinese society has emphasized the primacy of the family and the obligation of the individual to submerge personal ambition and goals for the sake of the harmony and prosperity of the family. Patricia Ebrey's article on family instructions shows that the rules governing families were extensive. These rules were taken from the preface of a late Ming dynasty (1368–1644) genealogy, but similar rules existed in earlier times, and the values expressed in these rules still influence Chinese society. These rules expressed an idealized view of how the family should function, but the prohibitions they contain also indicate the areas of potential conflict within the family.

The excerpt from Ba Jin's (Pa Chin's) novel, *The Family,* which is set in the early twentieth century, illustrates how the needs of the family determined the fate of Kao Chueh-hsin. In keeping with the hierarchical organization of the traditional Chinese family, Chueh-hsin's father and grandfather chose his education, wife, and occupation. Although Chueh-hsin did not welcome these decisions, he submitted to them, sadly but without objection. Despite Chueh-hsin's lack of freedom, the story seems to indicate that, at least in his marriage, Chueh-hsin was not entirely unhappy.

Wang Yalin and Li Jinrong's report on the urban worker's housework details the problems of contemporary life in urban China. Domestic chores continue to consume an incredible amount of time, burdening the personal lives of urban Chinese families, especially the women, and affecting the economy as well. Although the study does not address the issue directly, it would seem to indicate that the family will continue to be an important economic as well as social unit in contemporary China. Aside from the interesting findings contained in this study, the report is also significant because it was one of the first empirical sociological studies in post-1949 China.

Turning to family life, Mary Sheridan provides a poignant portrayal of Zhao Xiuyin, an industrious and intelligent peasant woman. Although Xiuyin was married in 1950 when equality for women had been established by law, pressure from her husband, which Xiuyin attributed to his "feudal attitudes," and the burdens of child-rearing prevented her from pursuing a career. Thus, despite official efforts to guarantee equality, traditional attitudes toward women still prevail in rural China, and women, such as Xiuyin, often fail to realize their ambitions. Quite often women are expected to undertake the same duties as men in addition to their traditional household work rather than instead of it.

Emily Honig tells the story of Yu Luojin, which depicts not only the persistence of traditional values, but also the changes that have occurred in contemporary Chinese society. Concern for the welfare of her family was an important consideration in Yu Luojin's decisions, though she ultimately did not lose sight of her own goals. Her experiences fall well short of the idyllic picture of marriage in contemporary China portrayed in the video "Marrying." The tyranny of tradition may have been overcome, but Yu Luojin's case shows that in contemporary China politics can, as tradition once did, impinge harshly on the personal choices of Chinese men and women.

The Marriage Law of 1950 ostensibly eliminated many of the traditional marriage customs that discriminated against women. Most notably, it provided for freedom of choice in marriage and gave women the right to divorce. In the video "Marrying," we see the effects of these reforms juxtaposed with the strength of traditional customs. The marriage shown in the video is one of free choice, but in deference to the bride's mother an intermediary is employed to obtain her permission. This intermediary also handles the complex negotiations for the gift-giving and the arrangements for the elaborate feasting which accompanies the wedding ceremony. Also in accordance with tradition, the bride marries into her husband's household. Although the relative advances for women have been among the most revolutionary changes since 1949, the tenacity of traditional attitudes toward women and the limits of the reform are evident, to varying degrees, in the video as well as in the lives of Zhao Xiuyin and Yu Luojin.

Key Concepts

Filial Piety. Filial piety refers to the first and most important of the five relationships of Confucianism, which is respect for one's parents. See "The Five Relationships" in Unit 3.

Lineage. A lineage is a corporate group that celebrates ritual unity and is based on demonstrated descent from a common ancestor. When the line of descent is traced through male members of the lineage, it is called a patrilineage. These are the units Westerners have called Chinese "clans."

Communes. Prior to 1984, the commune was the basic administrative unit in rural China. There were over 50,000 communes in China in 1980. The average size was 15,000 people or 3,000 families. The commune was responsible for registry of births and marriages, postal services, and police. Most communes also had a clinic and middle school. The commune also supervised procurement of grain to meet the state's agricultural delivery obligations and was the locus of political leadership in the countryside. The reforms of the 1980s eliminated the communes as administrative units and replaced them with townships.

Production Brigade. Prior to 1984, the production brigade was a political and economic unit in rural China that ranked just below the commune. On the average, each brigade included 1,000 people or 200 families. The brigade often administered a primary school and medical station. It played an intermediate role in negotiating agricultural production and delivery plans between teams and higher authorities. As a result of the 1980s reforms, most brigades were renamed administrative villages.

Production Team. Prior to 1984, the production team was a unit of 50 families or 100 to 250 people and was based on a small hamlet or a neighborhood within a larger village. Team leaders made the day-to-day decisions on farming and recorded the team members' work points, which determined individual shares of the team income. In most localities, this administrative level is no longer officially recognized, and peasant families once again farm on their own account, without team leader commands and work points.

Work Points. Prior to the rural economic reforms, members of production teams were assigned work points according to the particular tasks they performed. Work points were totaled up by the team accountant and were used to determine the shares of the collective income paid to each family. The value of each work point was based on the net team income divided by the total number of work points earned by all members.

Marriage Law of 1980. The Marriage Law of 1980 was essentially a continuation of the Marriage Law of 1950, which granted freedom of choice in marriage, granted women the right to divorce, outlawed the selling of brides, and banned many traditional marriage customs that discriminated against women. The Marriage Law of 1980 raised the legal age for marriage from 18 to 20 for females and from 20 to 22 for males. It also further liberalized divorce procedures and restated that children had the legal obligation to provide for their parents in old age.

Cultural Revolution. See Unit 1.

Review Questions

1. In what ways was the Chinese family viewed as the key to a good society, according to Whyte's introductory essay?

2. According to Whyte, what has been the attitude of the government toward the family since 1949?

3. As presented in "Family Instructions," what are the special responsibilities of parents? Of youngsters? What is the hierarchy or order of priority within lineages and families?

4. In the excerpt from Ba Jin's book *The Family,* what were Chueh-hsin's own aspirations, and why was he unable to realize them?

5. What was Chueh-hsin's attitude toward the frustration of his own goals, and how did he resolve this conflict in his life?

6. According to the article by Wang and Li, what are the causes of the high expenditure of time on housework in contemporary urban China?

7. What are the effects of the burden of housework on the individual? On society?

8. According to Mary Sheridan's article, what were the limitations on Xiuyin's life because of the "feudal" attitudes of her family and her husband?

9. How did life in Xiuyin's village change for women after Liberation?

10. According to Emily Honig's article, what political factors were involved in Yu Luojin's two marriages?

11. What were the differing points of view about "mutual affection" or love in marriage that were debated in Yu Luojin's second divorce case? What was her "radical definition"?

12. According to the video "Marrying," what are some of the major differences in attitudes toward women and marriage between traditional China and the official policies of China today?

13. What elements of the traditional wedding ceremony do the couple in "Marrying" retain? What is the official attitude toward such traditions today? Why does the couple choose to follow tradition?

Unit 6: Creating a Broader Community

Video: "Caring"

Readings

Introduction to Part 3, by Martin K. Whyte

31. "Urban Social Control," by Sybille van der Sprenkel
32. "The Commune as a Social System," by Martin K. Whyte
33. "A Chinese Hospital," by Gail E. Henderson and Myron S. Cohen
34. "My Neighborhood," by B. Michael Frolic
35. "Connections," by Zheng Yefu

Learning Objectives

To become acquainted with:

— traditional and modern forms of community and grass-roots organizations

— the importance of the work unit *(danwei)* in Chinese society

— the traditional and renewed use of personal "connection" *(guanxi)* networks

— the structure and function of neighborhood committees in urban China

— the organization of health care and social welfare services

Overview

Although Chinese families and kin groups sometimes act as if they were islands unto themselves, cooperation outside of the family has nonetheless been important. To illustrate China's heritage of social organization, this unit begins with Sybille van der Sprenkel's discussion of two types of unofficial organizations, guilds and temple associations, during the Qing dynasty (1644–1911). Such unofficial organizations, which arose among common-interest groups, coexisted with a territorial network of official, centralized organizations for exercising imperial authority. Temple associations were responsible for the maintenance of local temples, but they also served political, economic, and social functions. The fact that members shared religious beliefs enforced the authority of their leadership and provided a basis for resolving disputes among members. Guilds were largely responsible for the economic activities of townspeople, including establishing standards appropriate to their businesses and adjudicating disputes among members. The state could intervene in the economy, but detailed regulation was usually left to the guilds. Van der Sprenkel's article thus highlights the importance in traditional China of group solidarity and the interplay between official and unofficial social organization.

Rural areas had similar systems of local organization, including self-help and religious groups, as Martin K. Whyte points out in his Introduction to Part 3. The Chinese Communist revolution was based in the countryside, and it was rural China that experienced the most sweeping changes after 1949. The program of land reform begun in Communist base areas prior to 1949 ultimately led to the elimination of the small but powerful landlord class that had previously controlled rural society. In his selection in the text, "The Commune as a Social System," Whyte sketches the development of the new system of rural administration after 1949. During the early 1950s, the government began first to encourage and then to require the consolidation of individual landholdings into ever-larger cooperatives that were designed to pool tools and animals and regulate labor exchanges. The form of rural organization—communes, brigades, and production teams—that eventually took shape was consolidated by 1962. Significant policy changes after 1980 modified this structure. In an effort to spur agricultural production, the state granted production teams more autonomy, employed economic incentives, expanded free markets, and contracted farm land to individual families. These changes are discussed in more detail in Part 4. Eventually, the administrative terminology was changed, with township and village governments replacing communes and brigades, and the team in most cases disappearing as a recognized unit.

Contemporary social organization in urban China is examined in the article by Gail Henderson and Myron Cohen, who lived for six months in a provincial hospital. This selection examines the role of the work unit *(danwei)* as they experienced it in that hospital. In the early 1950s the government restricted migration to urban areas and centralized control over job and housing assignments. All workplaces in urban China were organized into administrative units. Each urban worker is assigned to a work unit that serves social, political, and economic functions. Although each work unit is under the jurisdiction of a higher bureaucratic unit, each remains relatively isolated, and contact between units can be problematic.

Another form of urban organization is described in B. Michael Frolic's article on neighborhood committees, which demonstrates how effective the extension of official government organization to the grassroots levels has been in China. The neighborhood committee is an arm of higher level political control, but it is also a means by which a community administers itself. In many ways it is similar to the unofficial organizations described by van der Sprenkel. Unlike traditional forms of local control, however, it is more tightly linked to the state, and each committee is supervised by the Public Security Bureau, although the neighborhood committee is staffed almost entirely by local residents. It is clear from this article how essential this form of social organization is to the maintenance of order and community well-being in China's cities.

Zheng Yefu's essay introduces us to the importance of "connections" *(guanxi)* in Chinese society. The use of connections—based on family ties, school ties, common geographic origin, or other particularistic ties—has a long history in China. According to Zheng, this reliance on connections is a part of the undesirable residue of China's past, whose abuse has been exacerbated by economic shortages and a loss of spiritual morality brought about by the Cultural Revolution. Zheng proposes the establishment of a rational legal system coupled with a renewal of spiritual morality as a solution to the reliance on connections. The continual shortages of adequate housing and the limited availability of medical and some consumer goods, however, provide the type of environment in which the reliance on connections seems unavoidable. Rejecting Western materialism, Zheng urges a new morality that will maintain the Chinese feeling for human relationships and create a modern, distinctively Chinese ethic and social order.

Time-honored concerns, such as orientation toward the group rather than the individual, respect for order, and trust in authority, continue to permeate modern China's urban social organization. As the video "Correcting" illustrates, these concerns prevail in mental hospitals and prisons, which are strikingly similar in their emphasis on conformity and reforming "incorrect" attitudes, thoughts, and behavior. The workings of the neighborhood committees also have resonances within China's past. For example, elderly women constitute a majority on most neighborhood committees and seem to have assumed the moral authority that matriarchs once had in traditional extended Chinese families. The continued importance of the family and the group as opposed to the individual is striking. As in the past, neighborhoods continue to share group responsibility for local order. This has been a hallmark of Chinese society, but it often comes at the expense of personal initiative and individuality.

Key Concepts

Danwei. In the early 1950s all workplaces in urban China were organized into *danwei* or administrative units. Each urban worker is assigned to a work unit that serves social, political, and economic functions. The unit assigns housing and access to social services and is also the center for discussion of local and national concerns.

Neighborhood Committees. The neighborhood committee (also referred to as residents' committee) is an arm of higher level political control, but it is also a means by which a community administers itself. Most of the members are local residents, usually retired women. Neighborhood committees settle local disputes, monitor neighborhood security, maintain buildings, and provide information on public health and birth control. They are closely supervised by Public Security cadres who work in the local police station.

Responsibility System. A major feature of the recent economic reforms, the responsibility system, has replaced collectivized farming in the countryside. Under this system individual households contract land from the state and assume the responsibility of supplying a specified amount of their output, at fixed prices, to the state. Surplus production remains under the control of the individual family and can be sold on the free market. In the past, all land was farmed collectively and the surplus was divided among members of production teams. Current reforms call for a responsibility system in industry as well. Workers would be responsible for a specified amount of production and would be rewarded with bonuses for surplus production. Failure to fulfill quotas would also be grounds for dismissal.

Iron Rice Bowl. Traditionally, the Chinese referred to their means of earning a livelihood as a "rice bowl." Under today's socialist system, the "iron rice bowl," which cannot be broken, serves as a metaphor for total job security. The post-1978 reforms have tried to eliminate this security as a way of promoting incentive, but so far with only limited success.

Guanxi. The Chinese term *guanxi* literally means "relationships," but in the present context it is better translated as "connections." The use of personal connections, such as family ties, school ties, and common places of origin, to obtain favors, bureaucratic advancement, or cement political ties has a long history in China.

Review Questions

1. What kind of rural organization existed in traditional China, according to Whyte's introductory essay?

2. What were the two traditional kinds of social control, as described by van der Sprenkel in her article on nineteenth-century imperial China?

3. What were two traditional types of social groups described by van der Sprenkel, and how did these associations provide order and community in towns?

4. Describe the basic functions of each administrative level of the commune system, as discussed by Whyte.

5. What were the different methods by which income was distributed in the commune system, according to Whyte?

6. What is a *danwei,* and what traditional social, political, and economic functions does it have, as described by Henderson and Cohen?

7. What are the structure and functions of the residents' committee, as described in "My Neighborhood"?

8. What opinions did the neighborhood committee members form about urban community organization in China, as compared to that in Hong Kong?

9. What are *guanxi,* and why are they so integral a part of traditional Chinese society? What does Zheng Yefu mean by a "personalized ethic"?

10. What causes does Zheng Yefu cite for the reemergence of "connections," and what suggestions does he make for eliminating reliance on them?

11. What are some of the basic, and distinctively Chinese, attitudes toward children, old people, community, medicine, mental health, and treatment of criminals as portrayed in the video "Caring"? How do these contrast with Western attitudes?

12. How have social changes affected traditional Chinese family and community life?

13. What major reason is given in the video for the current problem of disaffected youth?

Unit 7: Cleavages and Social Conflicts

Video: "Mediating"

Readings

Introduction to Part 3, by Martin K. Whyte

36. "Subethnic Rivalry," by Harry J. Lamley

37. "The Position of Peasants," by Sulamith Heins Potter
38. "The Class System of Rural China," by Jonathan Unger
39. "Birth Control: A Grim Game of Numbers," by Steven W. Mosher
40. "Saturday Night in Baoding," by Richard Terrill

Learning Objectives

To become acquainted with:

— some sources of social conflict in imperial China

— the restrictions and disabilities associated with peasant status

— social discord caused by the use of "class labels" and political criteria for advancement

— problems associated with enforcement of birth control policies

— the reappearance of social conflict resulting from reforms of rural organizations

— the role of mediation committees in divorce and other social problems

Overview

Respect for authority and the maintenance of social harmony have always been highly valued in China. Nevertheless, as in other societies, ethnic and religious differences in China have sometimes been sources of social cleavages and violence. Lamley's reading discusses the violence between subethnic groups in Taiwan during the eighteenth century, when Taiwan was still a frontier area. Many of the settlers came from areas in the southeast where subethnic differences, in this case primarily between Hokkien and Hakka groups, had long been a source of violence. Within each rival group common geographic origin, family and clan ties, and ethnic background provided cohesion. Violence was frequently highly organized and took place on such a large scale that government intervention was required to restore peace.

Another important cleavage within Chinese society today occurs between urban and rural households. Sulamith Heins Potter's essay on the position of peasants describes the disadvantages and limitations of rural residence. Under the Household Registration Act of 1959, residency status is ascribed at birth, thus effectively prohibiting legal migration to urban areas. Despite decades of Maoist praise of peasant life, the preference for urban living is apparent both in the urban resident's dread of being sent down to the countryside and in the peasant's envy of the comforts and opportunities of urban life.

According to the *Communist Manifesto,* written by Karl Marx and Friedrich Engels, "The history of all hitherto existing society is the history of class struggle." The concept of class struggle and a class-based analysis of society were two elements of Marxist ideology basic to Mao's thought. Unlike Western Marxists, however, Mao believed that class conflict could continue after the establishment of socialism. Jonathan Unger describes the application and consequences of the use of class labels in post-1949 China in association with land reform policies and the effort to dismantle the traditional socioeconomic structure of Chinese society. Discrimination based on bad class background was common in the past, but the post-1978 leadership has repudiated this aspect of Maoist thought.

The urgency and potential excesses of China's drive to control the population by stringent measures limiting family size are evident in the reading by Steven Mosher. As his account demonstrates, recent government intrusions into family life can be traumatic and sometimes result in violence. The strength of traditional values regarding family and children presents a formidable obstacle to the one-child policy. This problem is particularly severe in rural China, where the absence of social security for the aged, along with opportunities created by the new reforms, add an economic incentive for having large families. The video "Mediating" further illustrates some of the problems associated with the one-child birth control policy, which range from divorce to female infanticide. As the video reveals, when the dictates of policy confront traditional values, the consequences can be disastrous. The social pressure to conform that local mediation committees bring to bear can be overwhelming and—as the reconciliation in the video seems to show—effective.

As Richard Terrill's memoir demonstrates, despite the "liberalization" of political life described by Harding in Part 2, the Communist Party retains control over such fundamental decisions as job assignments for college students. According to Terrill's account, the system rewards those who toady to Party secretaries and arbitrarily divides students from loved ones and family. The failure to remedy such iniquities and to address the concerns of students is another example of the limitations of reform. Complaints over the lack freedom of choice in their personal lives were a recurrent theme in student demonstrations in the 1980s.

Key Concepts

Household Registration System. Under the Household Registration Act of 1959, residence—either urban or rural—is ascribed at birth. Peasants are designated as rural personnel, which means that they are not eligible to take jobs or live in urban areas. In his article, Jonathan Unger refers to this situation as birth-ascribed stratification.

State's Rice. This term is used by Chinese peasants in reference to the food available to urban workers. Unlike peasants who grow their own grain, urban workers purchase rice from the state at subsidized prices.

Going Down to the Countryside. During the Cultural Revolution many intellectuals, Party members (including Deng Xiaoping), and urban youth were sent down to the countryside to perform manual labor, in what amounted to a program of labor reform. Ostensibly, this policy was designed to bridge the gap between urban and rural China, but more often it was considered a form of punishment. Despite efforts to correct it, some victims of this policy are still unable to reestablish their urban residency.

Class Labels. In the early 1950s each household in China was ascribed a class label based on its pre-1949 socioeconomic status. Members of revolutionary classes, such as peasants and workers, received good class labels, while former capitalists or landlords were considered bad class elements. Such labels were particularly important during the process of land reform. For example, households designated as landlord class had much of their land confiscated. These class labels became fixed so that future generations continued to bear the stigma of a bad class label regardless of their current socioeconomic class.

One-Child Policy. In an effort to limit population growth, the Chinese government adopted a policy of one child per family in 1979. Under this policy families who agree to the one-child limit are rewarded with a variety of benefits, such as better access to health care and educational facilities. Similarly, there are penalties for families who exceed the one-child limit. To date the policy has been successful in urban areas, but it has met resistance in the countryside where there are economic advantages to larger families.

Native Place Associations. During imperial times native place associations were present in most large Chinese cities. These associations were usually organized according to provincial or county origin, and they served as meeting places and hostels for travelers, usually merchants.

Guilds. Guilds were a form of urban social organization made up of persons engaged in the same business or craft. The primary function of guilds was to establish local control over a profession or craft by setting standards of workmanship and price, protecting the business from competition, and settling disputes among guild members.

Liberal and Statist Options. During the Republican period (1912–1949) Chinese intellectuals and politicians offered a variety of visions of China's future. Martin Whyte, in his introductory essay, refers to these as the "liberal" and "statist" options. According to Whyte, the liberal option advocated the development of a modern state machinery, a well-developed legal system, an extensive marketing system, and the freeing of individuals from the excessive demands of and loyalties to their families and other social groups. The "statist" option advocated many of the same goals, but its distinctive feature was the belief that individual freedom from group constraints was very dangerous, with chaos the likely result. The proper solution was not to free individuals from the demands of families and personalistic groups, but to change the nature of these groups so that they would work to the benefit of society. It should be noted that advocates of the liberal option were largely intellectuals with little, if any, political power.

Review Questions

1. What might be some of the undesirable consequences of the post-Mao reforms, according to Whyte's Introduction?

2. As discussed in the Lamley article, what factors determined the composition of the feuding groups in Taiwan during the Qing (Ch'ing) period, and what organizations were the focus of these groups?

3. What political and economic reasons does Lamley give for the factional disputes?

4. What were the historical circumstances surrounding the establishment of the "Regulations for Household Registration," as given in the Potter article?

5. How did the regulations affect peasants as compared to workers? What effects did the regulations have on the relations between the two groups?

6. What reasons are given in the Unger article for the system of class labels established in the early 1950s?

7. Why were class label policies discarded after Mao's death?

8. As recounted in the Mosher article, what arguments did the cadres use to get women to "think clear" about abortions? What methods of persuasion did they use?

9. What factors influence the Party's assignment of jobs for college graduates? How does the process affect the students, according to Terrill?

10. Why have Chinese families traditionally wanted a large number of children, especially sons?

11. Why is the population control issue so important to the state?

12. What methods and appeals do the mediators use in the case illustrated in the video? How does the attitude of the mediators toward this family rift and potential divorce reflect Chinese values?

Essay/Discussion Questions for Part 3

1. Discuss traditional attitudes toward the individual in the Chinese family, and the extent to which these attitudes have—or have not—changed in contemporary China.

Suggested guidelines:

a. Consider the role of the family and its hierarchy, referring especially to:

- Whyte's Introduction
- the selections by Ebrey, Ba Jin, and Sheridan
- the function of the matchmaker in the video "Marrying"

b. Refer to the role of the government since 1949 as discussed in:

- Whyte's Introduction
- Honig's essay, especially concerning policies during the Cultural Revolution and the divorce debate
- Sheridan's account of the role of the village production team

c. Contrast the marriage situations of Chueh-hsin in Ba Jin's story and Yu Luojin in Honig's essay.

d. Consider the relationship between men and women, referring to:

- the housework burden in the study by Wang Yalin and Li Jinrong
- Sheridan's account of Zhao Xiuyin's marriage
- the videos "Marrying" and "Mediating"
- the definition of the basis of marriage by Yu Luojin's opponents

2. How has community organization since 1949 changed from imperial times? Consider both rural and urban areas, and both the Mao and post-Mao eras.

Suggested guidelines:

a. Consider the traditional roles of government, family, and the social network, referring to:

- van der Sprenkel's discussion of imperial control and urban groups, and Zheng Yefu's discussion of "connections"
- Terrill's article, concerning job assignments for college students
- Whyte's Introduction, on the subject of nonfamily groups and social networks
- Lamley's discussion of subethnic groups

b. Consider the effects of the reforms since 1949, referring to:

- the introduction to Part 3, discussing the aims and dilemmas of the state under and after Mao
- the Whyte article on communes and the Sheridan article "Zhao Xiuyin: Lady of the Sties," with attention to the relation of the family unit to socialist rural organization and the factors affecting the solidarity of the rural social system
- "A Chinese Hospital," concerning the functions and organization of the *danwei*
- the Frolic selection and the role of the residents' committees
- Zheng Yefu's discussion of the increased reliance of the Chinese on "connections"
- the videos "Caring" and "Mediating" on the relationships among family, individuals, and the state

3. What cleavages in China's social order have been generated as a result of changing Communist Party policies?

Suggested guidelines:

a. Consider policies that have directly affected families and individuals, referring to:

• the video "Mediating" and the Mosher article, comparing traditional attitudes toward family size and current state problems and policies regarding population

• Whyte's Introduction, concerning the effect of post-Mao economic reforms on decisions among individuals and neighbors

b. Consider how state policies have affected relations between subgroups, and between classes. Refer to:

• the Potter article—what does "eat the state's rice" mean, and what does the phrase reflect about the effect of the classification system on social cohesion?

• the Lamley and Potter articles, concerning tension between traditional rural subgroups

• Unger's article and his suggestion of why and how authorities have encouraged "scapegoating"

c. Consider how official policies have affected people's attitudes toward the state, referring to:

• the Introduction by Whyte, concerning expectations since the revolution

• Maoist and post-Mao policies as discussed in Whyte's Introduction. How do they compare?

Part 4

The Economy

Part 4 introduces us to the economy of China, focusing on agriculture, industry, and trade in imperial and Communist China. This section of the course highlights the methods, progress, and remaining problems of China's drive to modernize its economy.

Unit 8: Agriculture

Video: "Living"

Readings

Introduction to Part 4, by Robert F. Dernberger

41. "The Chinese Peasant Economy," by Ramon H. Myers
42. "Marketing and Social Structure in Rural China," by G. William Skinner
43. "The Commune System before Reform," by Frederick W. Crook
44. "Socialist Agriculture is Dead; Long Live Socialist Agriculture!" by Kathleen Hartford
45. "China's New Rural Reform Experiments," by Francis C. Tuan

Learning Objectives

To become acquainted with:

— peasant life in China, past and present

— the economic and political organization of rural China

— the marketing and social structure of rural China

— the effects and possible implications of economic reforms in the countryside

— the responsibility system and its impact on the rural economy

— the present state and future requirements of agricultural technology

Overview

The video "Living" introduces us to the Chinese peasantry, who make up about half of the Chinese population. Centuries of hard work have altered the landscape of China, enabling Chinese agriculture to support an ever-growing population. In some ways the life of the peasant has changed very little, since Chinese agriculture today remains highly labor-intensive, and much of the work done still relies on human labor. Nevertheless, changes have occurred in the economic and social organization of the rural sector. Peasants have benefited from increased access to education, medical care, and rural electrification. In contrast to the past, the government has played a much more active role in organizing peasants to build the rural infrastructure and to increase productivity. During the 1950s these efforts were sometimes counterproductive, but under the current responsibility system productivity has increased and living standards have risen. As in the past, the family has reemerged as the basic economic unit.

The selection by Ramon Myers is based on village studies carried out by the Japanese during their occupation of North China in the 1930s. The deterioration of the rural economy and the breakdown of rural society during the twentieth century, and its political implications, have been the subject of much debate among China scholars. Myers' examination of the data for several villages in North China finds that the effects of economic depression and war were variable. Throughout this period agricultural productivity kept pace with population growth, and peasant households, which remained the basic economic and social unit, responded rationally to changing economic circumstances. According to Myers, the government's failure to provide adequate education and support for technological development and lack of government support for increasing the supply of modern inputs for agricultural producers were the major impediments to the growth of agricultural output. Some specialists, on the other hand, have argued that the commercialization of Chinese agriculture, a process exacerbated by imperialism, sharply skewed the distribution of wealth in favor of the richer classes who did not reinvest in agriculture and engendered increased conflict between landowners and peasants.

Skinner's article provides a perspective on the agricultural marketing system. Skinner applies the principles of central place theory, combined with his own fieldwork in Sichuan, to delineate the limitations the marketing structure imposed on the development of Chinese agriculture. According to his findings, the high cost of transportation and transaction costs limited the size of the market system, thus restricting the development of Chinese agriculture.

As mentioned above, after 1949 a revolutionary program of land reform was implemented, and China's agricultural sector underwent extensive institutional reorganization. This was the most immediate and far-reaching result of the Communist revolution. The commune structure of political and economic organization that emerged is the subject of the chapter by Frederick Crook. The overall results were favorable, but at times the penetration of the government into rural society meant misguided and harmful interference in agriculture. He notes that artificial administrative boundaries, the centralization of administrative and economic decision-making, and the lack of economic incentives limited agricultural productivity.

In 1978 institutional organizations were reformed once again to grant greater freedom to individual families. Hartford's article outlines the benefits of the new organizational reforms, but also notes the need for technological inputs. In a sharp departure from Maoist models, peasants now contract land from the state and are essentially self-employed. Under this system peasants have prospered. Autonomy is limited, however, and peasants are still obligated to sell a portion of their produce to the state. Similarly, the peasant must still rely on the state to provide investment capital for the new technology that is necessary if agricultural productivity is to continue to increase.

Written in the early 1980s, Hartford's article anticipated many of the problems that arose during the latter half of the decade. As Hartford presciently noted, much of the increased output of the early 1980s was due to the one-time benefit of a shift in organization from collective to household agriculture. According to Dernberger, crop production stagnated after 1984 because the Chinese leadership was unwilling to achieve sustained growth through continuous price increases. Foregoing price increases as a means to stimulate production, the need for modern technology and large-scale irrigation becomes more urgent. Paradoxically, collective agriculture would be better suited to spreading modern technology and constructing large-scale irrigation projects; but, as Francis Tuan's report shows, the government was unwilling to recollectivize agriculture in the late 1980s. Instead, new experiments were proposed to remedy problems encountered in reform. These have included higher government procurement prices for grain (despite reforms, most grain is still sold to the state at fixed prices), promotion of private marketing and production cooperatives, and revamping the official credit and financial systems. As Dernberger points out, rural reform has met widespread popular approval, and the current leadership has relied on rural areas for political support in the wake of the Tiananmen Massacre. Consequently, there are strong economic and political incentives to continue rural reform.

Key Concepts

Technologist and Distributionalist Explanations of Constraints on Agriculture. Western scholars have offered many different explanations of why China's agricultural economy failed to achieve a successful transition to the high yields of modern scientific agriculture. Ramon Myers' article is an example of the technologist argument, which blames the failure of the government and educational system to make modern technology available to the peasants. Distributionalists argue that commercialization of agriculture in the twentieth century led to a worsening of income distribution between owners of land and tillers of land. According to this explanation, those who had the capital to invest in technology were using these funds for investment in other sectors or for the consumption of luxuries, while the poorer peasants lacked the means to invest in modern technology.

Production Responsibility System. The production responsibility system for agriculture was first introduced in 1978. Although its form may vary, it has retained two common features: production contracts between production teams and smaller units below the teams—usually households—and differential compensation distinguishing the work contribution of each producer. In most cases individual households contract land from the state. Production teams retain a role in centralized production planning, but day-to-day management devolves to individual households.

Specialized Household. The contracting of land to individual households has led to a more efficient use of labor, which in turn has produced a surplus labor force in the countryside. To remedy this problem rural cadres have arranged contracts with peasants whose special productive skills require little or no land, such as beekeeping or livestock-raising, or individuals may enter small-scale production, repair work, or commerce using their own investment funds. Such households are known as specialized households.

Review Questions

1. According to Dernberger's Introduction, what is the nature, and what are the causes, of China's current population problem?

2. What features of China's traditional economic system accounted for the success of Chinese agriculture in the eighteenth and nineteenth centuries, according to Dernberger?

3. What reasons does Myers give for the maintenance of living standards despite population increases? What inputs does he cite as necessary to improve agricultural production?

4. What is the spatial model of the hierarchical system of the traditional market structure, as described by Skinner?

5. What are the functions of the standard and intermediate markets, respectively? How do they form a societywide economy?

6. According to the Crook article, how did the aims of the commune system reflect Mao's vision of a socialist society? How was the system organized to implement Party aims in both economic goals and political behavior?

7. What is Crook's assessment of the strengths and weaknesses of the commune system?

8. What are the basic mechanisms of the responsibility system discussed in the Hartford article?

9. How, in Hartford's view, does the emerging new model for Chinese agricultural production retain the same root assumptions as the Maoist model?

10. What difficulties does Hartford see for the agricultural reforms? What does she think is necessary for China to break through its "developmental impasse" in agriculture?

11. What "experiments" has the government initiated in rural areas to remedy problems with the agricultural reforms of the late 1970s? According to Dernberger, what are some of the political considerations that have influenced rural reform?

12. As presented in the video "Living," what changes in official attitude are reflected in the new responsibility system? What worries China's leaders about recent economic gains?

13. As shown in the video, how has organizational innovation affected the villagers of Maoping? What are the duties of Mr. Fang, the Communist Party secretary in Maoping?

Unit 9: Industry

Video: "Working"

Readings

Introduction to Part 4, by Robert F. Dernberger

46. "The Foreign Establishment in China in the Early Twentieth Century," by Albert Feuerwerker
47. "China's Transition to Industrialism," by Thomas G. Rawski
48. "China: The Economic System," report by the World Bank
49. "China's Economic Reforms," by Robert F. Dernberger

Learning Objectives

To become acquainted with:

— the foreign economic presence in China in the twentieth century

— the impact of foreign enterprises on indigenous industrialization

— economic, especially industrial, development during the first half of the twentieth century

— the essential features of the Soviet economic model

— the scope of economic reform in China

Overview

Industrialization is a relatively recent phenomenon in China, which began only after the country was opened to foreign trade in the nineteenth century. Throughout the nineteenth century, foreign powers pressured the imperial government to open an increasing number of cities to foreign trade (see Unit 10: Trade). Within these cities, known as treaty ports, foreign businessmen were immune from Chinese law, and foreigners enjoyed special privileges, such as fixed customs duties, which were denied to their Chinese competitors. The humiliating manner in which China was opened to foreign trade during the period from 1840 to 1949 has left a bitter residue in the minds of many Chinese. In fact, some historians in China maintain that the intrusion of the militant Western commercial powers snuffed out indigenous capitalist development in late imperial China. While Western economists may approach the problem of China's early industrialization from a purely economic standpoint, for the Chinese it is often a deeply emotional issue involving national pride.

Chinese nationalists from both ends of the political spectrum have argued that the failure of China's early efforts to industrialize was due largely to the privileged status of foreign enterprises. One fact is clear: prior to 1949, foreign enterprises had played a dominant role in the development of the modern industrial sector in China. The impact of the foreign economic presence in China is the subject of a balanced essay by Albert Feuerwerker, which is sensitive to both the economic and political dimensions of this question. In his systematic examination of trade, banking, manufacturing and mining, transport, and public finance, he concludes that foreign economic gains were not an absolute deduction from China's economic welfare and that the psychological and political impact of the foreign presence had a far more significant effect on the course of China's modern history.

During the first half of the twentieth century, political turmoil, foreign competition, and war limited the growth of native Chinese industry. Nevertheless, Thomas Rawski's research reveals that during this period Chinese entrepreneurs and engineers developed skills that provided a base for industrial expansion after 1949. His study focuses on engineering firms, originally established to repair and service foreign machinery, and on the entrepreneurial skills that the Chinese learned from their foreign competitors. Thus, despite the apparent weakness of Chinese industry prior to 1949, significant gains were being made in several important areas. Rawski's essay is representative of the more detached, strictly economic evaluations of China's early industrialization.

After 1949 China turned to the Soviet Union for economic assistance and guidance. The locomotive factory featured in the video "Working" is just one example of Soviet economic aid. China's Communist leaders also adopted the Soviet economic model, which is the subject of the World Bank study included in the readings. Under this highly centralized system, the Communist Party determines economic policy, and the state manages the national economy; market forces have virtually no impact on economic decisions. Annual plans, based on administrative decisions, determine the flow of resources, prices, wages, and labor-power allocation. Inefficiencies have plagued the system, leading to increasing demands for reform.

The video "Working" introduces us to industrial life in China. Workers occupy a key economic and political position in Communist society, and the Chinese state is very sensitive to their needs and attitudes. Industrial jobs are highly prized, since they offer lifetime security and a wide range of social services. Yet the hazardous working conditions, long hours, and Party control depicted in the video reveal that the material rewards and political status of workers have their price. The future also poses questions for workers, as the responsibility system threatens to shatter the "iron rice bowls" of unproductive workers.

Robert Dernberger's article assesses the impact of the economic reforms that have been put into practice during the 1980s. These reforms — which include reduction of central planning, more autonomy for enterprise managers, creation of private and collectively owned enterprises to compete with state-owned enterprises, relaxation of state control over the allocation of goods and services, and price reform — have resulted in what Dernberger calls a "mixed economic system." Market forces have been allowed to play a greater role in the economy, but the state-owned sector continues to dominate. Although government controls have been relaxed, Chinese leaders insist that they will not allow a capitalist market system to take root in China. Further reforms will be difficult and will require political courage. For the time being, China's leaders seem determined to place political stability ahead of economic reform; but, as Dernberger points out, the example of Eastern Europe would seem to indicate that it will be difficult to stem the demand for both economic and political reform.

Key Concepts

State Enterprises. State-owned and -administered enterprises dominate the Chinese economy. The state appoints the management personnel, decides annual production targets, and determines wages and prices. There are also a number of private enterprises, including self-employment and workers collectives, that are nominally owned by their members. State enterprises now pay taxes, rather than remit the profits directly to the state, but are still administered by various state bureaus and agencies. Cooperatives and private enterprises have fewer direct ties to the state, but are often subject to control by local officials.

Soviet-Style Economic System. Under Stalin's leadership, in the 1920s and 1930s the Soviet Union developed economic policies and institutions designed to secure industrial development. The Soviet experience later became a model for other Communist countries. The Soviet model is characterized by the mobilization of a high rate of savings for the purpose of investing in production facilities for the heavy industrial sector. Resources and commodities are allocated according to plans and administrative directives implemented by a centralized bureaucracy.

Market Socialism. Market socialism is a term used to describe a socialist economy in which market forces, the law of supply and demand, play a major role in the allocation of resources and commodities. The extent to which market forces are a factor may vary, however. In the case of China, for example, the recent reforms have led to a relaxation of some features of the Soviet-style economic model described above, but the state still retains ownership of the means of production and control over the distribution of most resources.

Review Questions

1. According to Dernberger's Introduction, what factors inhibited the development of industry in China?

2. In what ways did the Chinese reorganize China's industrial sector after 1949, according to Dernberger's Introduction?

3. According to Feuerwerker, what were the political, economic, and psychological effects of the foreign presence in China?

4. In Feuerwerker's view, what were the factors responsible for China's slow economic growth before 1949?

5. In Rawski's selection in the text, how does he account for the growth of Chinese industries before 1937, which, in his view, laid a foundation for continuing development in the producer sector?

6. As documented in the World Bank study, what are the basic instruments of management of China's socialist economic system?

7. According to the World Bank report, how are jobs allocated in the Chinese economic system? What methods are used to remunerate workers in state organizations and urban collectives, including items of income support?

8. What is the relationship of China's domestic and export prices to the world market, as discussed in the World Bank report?

9. What are the three key aspects of economic reform that Dernberger discusses in his article? How successful have these reforms been?

10. How have political considerations affected economic reforms? What are the three major political groupings that Dernberger identifies among the reformers in China's government?

11. What are the advantages and disadvantages of being an industrial worker in China, as revealed in the video "Working"? How has the introduction of the responsibility system affected workers? What problems are being addressed by the state with this system?

Unit 10: Trade

Video: "Trading"

Readings

Introduction to Part 4, by Robert F. Dernberger

50. "Foreign Trade and Industrial Development of China," by Yu-kwei Cheng

51. "China's Balance of Payments in the Twentieth Century," by Nai-ruenn Chen

52. "Economic Modernization in Contemporary China: Limiting Dependence on Foreign Technology," by Robert F. Dernberger

53. "China's Open-Door Policy," by Sheree Groves

Learning Objectives

To become acquainted with:

— the conduct of foreign trade in traditional China

— the opening of China to foreign trade during the nineteenth century

— the unequal treaties and the development of the treaty port system

— the influence of politics on foreign trade policy after 1949

— recent reforms in the conduct of foreign trade

— the establishment of special economic zones

Overview

The Chinese have never looked upon foreign trade as simply an economic matter. Since the early days of the Silk Road, pictured in the video "Trading," Chinese emperors sought strict control over the conduct of foreign trade. Trade was often conducted under the guise of tribute missions to the emperor. Regardless of the actual circumstances, Chinese emperors welcomed foreign merchants as emissaries of foreign rulers wishing to bestow gifts in recognition of the supreme position of China's emperor. There were also more practical political reasons for closely monitoring foreign trade. Quite frequently such foreign ideas as Islam and Buddhism were imported along with foreign goods. Similarly, the imperial state recognized the potential political threat of a wealthy merchant class. Merchants were relegated to the lowest social status in imperial China, beneath scholars, peasants, and artisans.

For centuries the Chinese were able to exercise some degree of control over the flow of foreign trade, but this situation changed dramatically in the nineteenth century when China was confronted by the militant economic power of the West. Yu-kwei Cheng's article traces the evolution of the treaty port system that was imposed on China over the course of the nineteenth century. Prior to the Opium War in 1842, trade with the West was restricted to the southern port of Guangzhou (Canton). The Treaty of Nanjing, signed by China after its defeat by Britain, opened the way to greater foreign penetration of the Chinese economy and new concessions from the feeble imperial government. By the turn of the century, the foreign powers had divided China into exclusive spheres of influence, causing many observers to fear that Chinese sovereignty would be extinguished completely. Resentment of foreign imperialism fed nascent Chinese nationalism and gave birth to a broad range of political movements, which eventually combined to overthrow the Qing government in the Revolution of 1911.

Throughout the first half of the twentieth century China suffered from a large foreign trade deficit. Some scholars have argued that this deficit drained the Chinese economy of the capital needed for economic modernization. Nai-ruenn Chen's essay argues that the remittances from overseas Chinese laborers, businessmen, and entrepreneurs financed this deficit. Over time, he argues, the Chinese economy benefited from being able to import more commodities than were being exported. Chen, like Rawski, adopts a purely economic calculus to examine what is for the Chinese also an emotional and political issue. Although his argument may be sound economically, it is important to realize that very few Chinese at the time perceived the problem in these terms. Many Chinese continue to harbor bitter memories of the one-hundred-year history of imperialism in China, and this sentiment still influences contemporary debates over increasing foreign trade.

Since 1949 the Chinese attitude toward foreign trade has sometimes appeared contradictory. Economic policy has alternated between periods of self-reliance and periods of active borrowing of foreign technology. According to Robert Dernberger, this issue became a major point of contention among China's leaders, and the dramatic shifts in political power over the last 35 years are reflected in China's foreign trade patterns. In addition, he argues that an awareness of modern technology's potential to undermine political and social institutions, as it did in the late nineteenth century, has militated against a more open trade policy. The current regime is therefore concerned to limit the impact of China's opening to the outside world. As we see in the video "Trading," one solution has been to limit foreign investment to Special Economic Zones. Ironically, the most important of these zones is located not far from Guangzhou, where the foreign penetration of the Chinese economy began in the nineteenth century.

Despite the political turmoil of the late 1980s, China's leaders have never renounced the policy of opening to the outside world. Imports and exports have continued to expand rapidly, and the Chinese government has retained policies designed to encourage direct foreign investment. As the article by Groves explains, in addition to the Special Economic Zones in southern China, in 14 major coastal cities, from Dalian in the north to Guangzhou in the south, the government has provided special incentives to encourage foreign investment and technical cooperation. Another breakthrough came in 1987 when foreigners were permitted to purchase long-term land-use rights. However, since the violent crackdown on political dissent in 1989, direct foreign investment has slowed considerably. Whether or not this proves to be a temporary setback or a long-term downturn will depend in part on future political stability. Nevertheless, the fact that China became the largest foreign trader of any developing country during the 1980s would seem to indicate that the incentives to expand economic reforms do exist.

Key Concepts

Treaty Ports. Prior to the Opium War in 1842, foreign trade with China was limited to the southern port of Guangzhou (Canton), and the right to trade with foreigners was limited to licensed Chinese merchants known collectively as the *Co-Hong.* After the signing of the Treaty of Nanjing, the number of ports opened to foreign trade gradually increased. Since foreign trade was restricted to ports opened by treaty, they became known as treaty ports. The "most-favored-nation" provision soon became a feature of all commercial treaties concluded between China and the foreign powers. The most-favored-nation provision meant that whenever China granted additional rights and privileges to a foreign power, all other nations with most-favored-nation status automatically received the same rights and privileges. In contrast to the present-day usage of the most-favored-nation provision, however, foreign powers did not grant similar status to China.

Spheres of Influence. During the late nineteenth century, imperialist powers in China attempted to extend their economic rights and privileges through the establishment of spheres of influence. Unlike the colonial situation in Africa and other parts of Asia, although the imperialist powers exerted political and economic influence within their spheres of influence, actual political administration remained in Chinese control. These spheres of influence included: the British in the Yangzi valley, the French in south and southwest China, the Russians in northern Manchuria, the Germans in Shandong province, and the Japanese in southern Manchuria.

Open-Door Policy. The meaning of the "open-door policy" in China has changed since it was first proposed by the United States in the early twentieth century. At that time the United States feared that the creation of exclusive spheres of influence by the imperialist powers in China would undermine Chinese sovereignty and lead to exclusion of American products from the China market. Thus, the United States proposed an open-door policy that called for respect of Chinese sovereignty and equal economic opportunity for all foreign powers in China. At the time, the proposal received little support from other foreign powers, and many Chinese politicians denounced this policy as a justification for even greater foreign penetration of China's economy. Currently, the term "open-door policy" is used by the Chinese themselves to describe the reopening of China to foreign trade, in contrast to the "closed door" or autarkic policies of the Maoist era.

Autarky. Autarky is the policy of establishing a completely self-sufficient national economy independent of imports from other countries. While autarky was a cornerstone of Maoist economic policy beginning in the late 1950s, the United States trade embargo of China that began in 1949 and the cutoff in 1960 of Soviet aid (which had been an important component in Chinese economic development since 1949) left the Chinese little alternative but to pursue an autarkic policy. Since the normalization of relations between the United States and China and the abandonment of Maoist economic policies, foreign trade has grown rapidly as the Chinese seek foreign technology to aid in their modernization program.

Technological Imperative. Some social scientists have argued that modern technology determines certain policies and patterns of behavior. This process is known as the technological imperative. Technology that was developed in the West in a particular institutional environment might thus generate forces that undermine the institutions of a different environment or culture into which the technology is transferred. The Maoist emphasis on economic self-reliance was based partly on an awareness of this problem.

Special Economic Zones. In the post-Mao era of economic reform, the Chinese have established a series of special economic zones to attract foreign investors. Within these zones special tax incentives and preferential treatment with regard to land, raw materials, customs regulations, labor contracts, and foreign currency controls are granted to foreign investors. The major zones are located in the south near Hong Kong and in Fujian. Ordinary Chinese are not allowed access to these zones, thus limiting the impact of the foreign presence on the Chinese society and economy.

Review Questions

1. As discussed in the Yu-kwei Cheng article, what were the reasons for the Opium War, and what were its effects on China's relations with foreign powers?

2. What factors does Yu-kwei Cheng cite as having hampered the development of China's foreign trade?

3. What factors does Nai-ruenn Chen cite in his article as being responsible for the growth of Chinese imports, slow export growth, and the long-term deficit?

4. How, according to Nai-ruenn Chen, was China able to finance the persistent trade deficit from the end of the nineteenth century to 1940?

5. In what ways does Yu-kwei Cheng disagree with Nai-ruenn Chen's thesis that China's passive trade balance was counterbalanced by foreign remittances?

6. According to Dernberger's selection in the text, what has been the ambivalence in China's attitude toward economic relations with foreigners?

7. How did Mao view the problems generated by the importation of foreign technology? What advice did Mao give, and how, in Dernberger's view, has Mao's advice succeeded?

8. What incentives do Special Economic Zones provide for foreign investors? How have these types of incentives been extended to other areas?

9. As shown in the video "Trading," what were the effects on China of its early history of foreign trade?

10. How did the Cultural Revolution affect China's entrepreneurs, as shown in the video "Trading"? How have attitudes and policies changed since then, and for what reasons?

11. How have new policies affected social habits, especially in urban areas? Do you think fear of Westernization is well founded?

Essay/Discussion Questions for Part 4

1. What major problems have the different Communist systems of agricultural organization tried to solve? And how does the new responsibility system relate to the traditional system of agricultural production?

Suggested guidelines:

a. Review Dernberger's Introduction and the articles by Hartford and Tuan.

b. Consider the constraints on development in the agricultural sector, referring to:

- the headnote to the Skinner article, describing the "technologist" and "distributionalist" explanations for slow growth

- the Hartford and Myers articles, regarding the need for improved technology

- the Skinner discussion of traditional village-regional marketing structures, and the Hartford suggestion of a contradiction between comparative regional advantages and central planning

- the Crook and Hartford discussions, concerning motivational factors and income distribution

- Hartford's forecast of difficulties in the new model of socialist agriculture

- Tuan's article, regarding adjustments in the agricultural reforms

c. Consider the similarities and differences between the traditional system and the responsibility system, with reference to:

- Hartford's new model of socialist agriculture, as compared with Myers' description of traditional village organization, with attention to responsibilities for decisions affecting uses of land, labor, production, distribution, compensation, and labor-intensive organization

2. How have the Chinese Communists dealt with the need for modernization in the industrial sector of their economy?

Suggested guidelines:

a. Consider the state of the industrial sector they inherited, referring to:

- Feuerwerker and Rawski, and their arguments concerning the impact of the foreign presence on the economy

- the discussion of China's industrial revolution in Dernberger's Introduction

- Groves' discussion of Special Economic Zones

b. Review the Soviet model discussed in the headnote to the World Bank study and in the study itself, with attention to:

- tiered governmental structure

- enterprise plans and targets

- methods of determining money and commodity flows, and price controls

c. Consider the state's problems as seen in the video "Working" and its methods of dealing with them, with special attention to:

- motivation and training

- the conflict between full-employment policies and the need for greater efficiency

- the impact of the responsibility system

d. Consider Dernberger's analysis of the post-Mao reforms, especially in the areas of:

- the aims of the reforms

- the relationship among state, collective, and individually operated enterprises

- the contrast between guidance and mandatory planning

- the allocation of goods and services

- price determination and the relationship between centralized planning and market forces

3. What are the reasons for China's somewhat ambivalent attitude toward opening the country to foreign trade, and what effect has this ambivalence had on policy since 1949?

Suggested guidelines:

a. Consider the history of China's trade relations, referring to:

- Murphey's Introduction to Part 1 and the documents in Unit 1

- Yu-kwei Cheng's discussion in Unit 10, especially about the century of imperialism and China's efforts to restrict foreign trade

- the video "Trading," concerning foreign influences and Chinese historical attitudes toward foreigners

- Nai-ruenn Chen's article on the influences of the foreign powers on China's trade deficit from 1898 to 1940

- Yu-kwei Cheng and Nai-ruenn Chen's articles in Unit 10 and the articles by Feuerwerker and Rawski in Unit 9. Consider their different views of the economic effects of the foreign presence

b. How have the conflicting attitudes been reflected in radical shifts in the pattern of China's foreign trade? Refer to:

- Dernberger's discussion in the text of policy shifts, Mao and post-Mao attitudes toward the "technological imperative," and a policy of dual technological development (capital-intensive and labor-intensive)

c. Consider current policies, referring to:

- Groves' and Dernberger's discussions in the text of China's current aims and incentives for foreign economic activity

- the video "Trading," showing current attitudes toward Chinese capitalists and private enterprise, free markets, overseas Chinese, joint ventures, and concerns about the effects of foreign influence on Chinese culture and society

Part 5

Culture

Part 5 introduces two aspects of culture which, in traditional China, were highly integrated: literature and the arts, and science and technology. This section of the course focuses on trends in Chinese culture and on the relationship of the arts and of science and technology to the political and economic goals of China.

Unit 11: Literature and the Arts

Video: "Creating"

Readings

Introduction to Part 5, by Kenneth J. DeWoskin

54. "K'ung I-chi," by Lu Hsün
55. "Talks at the Yan'an Conference on Literature and Art," by Mao Zedong
56. "The Wounded," by Lu Xinhua
57. "Ancient Temple" and "In the Ruins," by Bei Dao
58. "People or Monsters?" by Liu Binyan

Learning Objectives

To become acquainted with:

— a broad survey of Chinese art and literature

— traditional Chinese approaches to art

— some themes in modern Chinese fiction

— the Maoist interpretation of the relationship between literature and the arts and revolution

— the impact of the Cultural Revolution on contemporary artists and writers

Overview

Four thousand years of Chinese civilization have yielded a rich tapestry of literature and art. A highly conservative elite education has supplied the foundation for the continuity of Chinese culture over the centuries. In fact widespread confrontation with Western culture did not occur until the early twentieth century, when China fought the efforts of the imperialist powers to carve her up into exclusive spheres of influence. The resulting reevaluation of traditional culture culminated in the May Fourth Movement, which spawned new movements in the arts and literature and gave impetus to the formation of many of China's modern political organizations, including the Communist Party. However, as the video "Creating" illustrates through the work and reflections of artists in different disciplines, Chinese artists have always been mindful of the work of their predecessors, and the resonances of the past continue to inform and guide the literature and art of the present. Despite greater openness to foreign influences, the arts in China retain qualities that are uniquely Chinese.

Chinese intellectuals and artists have always occupied an important and influential place in society. For this reason literature and art have often been subjected to careful scrutiny by China's rulers. In contemporary times, nowhere has the relationship between culture and politics been more clearly enunciated than in Mao Zedong's "Talks at the Yan'an Conference on Literature and Art." Mao's message was clear:

literature and art must serve the revolution. He urged artists and writers to learn from the masses and to produce a new literature and art that derived its content from popular life.

In the course of his talks, Mao praised Lu Xun (Lu Hsün), regarded as one of modern China's greatest writers of fiction. Lu was a member of the vanguard of Chinese writers who called for an abandonment of elite literary styles and the use of a vernacular style that could reach a wider audience. The sample of his work included in these readings is a satire of traditional intellectuals, designed to point out the weaknesses of traditional culture.

In the video "Creating," we meet several artists and writers who were victims of the Cultural Revolution. Traditionally, Chinese writers and artists have believed that their work should express their unalterable inner convictions. Thus the Cultural Revolution was particularly difficult for them, and today they are beginning to express the sufferings of this period in their work. Lu Xinhua's story is an example of the "Literature of the Wounded," stories of the emotional and personal consequences of the Cultural Revolution. Both the devastating personal effects of the Cultural Revolution and the remarkable resiliency of Chinese intellectuals are apparent in Bei Dao's melancholic work "In the Ruins."

During the 1980s it seemed that a new era of liberation in Chinese arts and literature was in the making. Throughout the decade, there were numerous indications that the government had become tolerant of artistic expression, and cultural exchanges and opportunities for Chinese artists and writers to travel abroad also increased markedly. Internally, the appearance of new forms of investigative reportage that exposed corruption in the Party and government, such as the work of Liu Binyan excerpted in the text, represented a dramatic breakthrough for the highly controlled Chinese press. New directions in literature, such as the poem "Ancient Temple" by Bei Dao, seemed to herald new vistas in both the content and form of Chinese literature. Most recently, the development of Chinese cinema gained international recognition when "Ju Dou," one of many excellent films produced in China during the 1980s, became the first Chinese film to be nominated for an

Academy Award. Unfortunately, since the Tiananmen Massacre the arts and literature have been subjected to greater government control.

Even before the bloody events of June 4, 1989, the Chinese government took some steps to reimpose control over intellectuals. For example, several leading writers, including Liu Binyan who now lives in exile in the United States, were denounced publicly and stripped of their Party memberships in 1987. The violent crackdown on political dissent in June 1989 has had a chilling impact on the arts and literature greater than anything since the Cultural Revolution. While this most recent crackdown was quite brutal during the initial stages, many Chinese intellectuals have reacted cynically and have at least passively resisted the efforts of the government to reimpose control over the arts. Government appeals to political orthodoxy and Chinese patriotism have failed to move Chinese intellectuals. While many intellectuals in China and abroad hope for swift return to the greater freedom enjoyed during the 1980s, conflict between artists and the state, and between the legacy of the past and the demands of the future, will likely influence art and literature for a long time to come.

Key Concepts

Qi. Qi, alternately translated as "configured energy" and "energetic configurations," is a vitalizing energy that is both universal and highly particular. *Qi* plays an important part in Chinese cosmological and metaphysical thought. At times it means the spirit of life in living creatures; at other times it is the air or ether surrounding the universe. In some contexts it denotes the basic substance of all creation.

May Fourth Movement. See Unit 1.

The Literature of the Wounded. The Literature of the Wounded is the work of a new generation of Chinese writers who came of age during the Cultural Revolution. Severely critical of the Gang of Four, their novels and stories represent a rigorous self-examination of the people who were caught up in the excesses of the Cultural Revolution. This body of work has been promoted by China's leaders, many of whom also suffered during the Cultural Revolution.

Misty Poetry. Misty Poetry is also called the "New Poetry of the New Chinese Generation." It is a movement dedicated to forging a new poetry free of the formal and contextual restraints of traditional Chinese poetry, as well as contemporary ideological restraints. Simultaneously, it also seeks a return to the ambiguity, nuance, and striking imagery of traditional work.

Review Questions

1. According to DeWoskin's Introduction, what constitutes the traditional concept of "culture" in China?

2. What was the role of literature and the arts in traditional Chinese society?

3. In the story "Kung I-chi," what is the author's attitude toward China's traditional culture, and how is this conveyed?

4. What did Mao claim, in his speech at the Yan'an Conference, to be the source of literature and art and the relationship of literature and art to politics?

5. What were Mao's stated attitudes toward ancient and foreign literature and art, and toward the individual artist?

6. Why do you think "The Wounded" has been considered a "flagship piece" of post–Cultural Revolution literature?

7. What seem to be the strengths and weaknesses of life in a collective, as depicted in "The Wounded"? What contradiction in Maoist thought, as presented in the story, affects Xiaohua's life?

8. In what ways did Liu Binyan's new journalistic style represent an important breakthrough in Chinese journalism?

9. How do the content and form of the "new poetry" differ from both traditional and revolutionary poetry? What aspects of the new poetry do Bei Dao's poems reveal?

10. As shown in the video "Creating," what Chinese religious and philosophic concepts have been important in Chinese arts? How does the Chinese view of "reality" compare with Western views?

11. As portrayed in the video "Creating," what has been the effect of Communist ideology in general, and of the Cultural Revolution in particular, on attitudes toward, and experiences of, artists in China? How have these conflicted with traditional attitudes?

Unit 12: Science and Technology

Video: "Understanding"

Readings

Introduction to Part 5, by Kenneth J. DeWoskin

59. "Chinese Science: Explorations of an Ancient Tradition," by Nathan Sivin

60. "Science in Contemporary China," by Leo A. Orleans

61. "National Plan for the Development of Science and Technology (1975–1985)," by Fang Yi

62. "*DOS ex Machina:* The Microelectronic Ghost in China's Modernization Machine," by Richard Baum

Learning Objectives

To become acquainted with:

— the historic contributions of Chinese science and technology

— several hypotheses to explain the arrested development of science in China

— the major branches of scientific study in traditional China

— the concepts of *yin* and *yang* in medicine and science

— the development of science in China since 1949

— the future goals of scientific and technological development in China

Overview

Given the recent history of Chinese scientific and technological development, it is easy to forget that as late as the seventeenth century Chinese science was unsurpassed by that of any other civilization. After all, the compass, gunpowder, paper, and printing were all invented in China. Nathan Sivin's article delineates the basic categories of early Chinese science: medicine, alchemy, astrology, geomancy, physical studies, and mathematics. He also makes the point that cultural perceptions have a great impact on scientific thought. One fundamental principle of early Chinese science was the belief that the natural world was governed by a balance of opposing forces called *yin* and *yang*. The Chinese believed that all changes occurring in nature were a result of the interplay of these two forces. The video "Understanding" presents several examples of how this principle was applied to medicine, astrology, and physical studies. The application of this principle in the practice of medicine continues to this day.

The video "Understanding" also shows a stunning example of how seismology has benefited from the blending of traditional and modern technology. Indeed, much of Chinese science has benefited from the longstanding Chinese respect for knowledge and scholarship. As discussed in the selection by Leo Orleans, which deals with post-1949 scientific development, Mao himself was a strong advocate of modern scientific research (although he also urged Chinese scientists to learn from the past). However, the Great Leap Forward and the Cultural Revolution slowed advances in scientific knowledge, and the closing of universities during the Cultural Revolution left a serious generation gap within the scientific community. To remedy this situation the state has invested more heavily in scientific development and provided more opportunities for scientists to study abroad. By promoting scientific research, China's leaders hope to increase economic output, upgrade national defense, and garner greater international recognition and prestige.

Thus, under the program of the Four Modernizations, the modernization of science has been designated as the key link that will propel advances in agriculture, industry, and national defense. As Fang Yi, former Minister of the State Science and Technology Commission, points out in his speech excerpted in the text, China urgently needs to improve virtually every area of scientific and technological study. The objectives spelled out in Fang's speech are ambitious and, some would say, represent a wish list more than a practical program for development. Nevertheless, some significant gains have already been made. For example, Chinese laser technology has advanced markedly in just a few years, and the Beijing Electron-Positron Collider was officially opened in late 1989.

Baum's article charts the development of the microcomputer industry in China over the past decade. Computer technology has been given a high priority in China's quest for modernization, and the gains in this field have been impressive. Despite formidable problems, including a lack of trained personnel and support networks, the difficulty of adjusting computers to accommodate the Chinese language, and inadequate maintenance and environmental controls, significant strides have been made in the production and dissemination of microcomputers. According to Baum, the microcomputer "boom," which began in the early 1980s, did not level off until 1986. The inventory of microprocessors jumped from 2,300 units in 1981 to about 100,000 by 1985. This was a substantial jump, though still small on a per-capita basis. The most encouraging news from a Chinese point of view has been the growing number of domestically produced computers. While most observers agree that there is tremendous potential for development, many also fear that the threat that the widespread use of microcomputers poses to the Chinese Communist Party's monopolistic control over the means of mass communication could be a major obstacle to future growth.

While Chinese science and technology made some impressive gains in the 1980s, the future is not entirely bright. In part this has been due to political events. Since the June 4 crackdown, many foreign governments have suspended or scaled down scientific exchanges with China. Chinese scholars abroad, the majority of whom are in the physical sciences, have also been reluctant to return to China. Many of the 40,000 students and visiting scholars in the United States have chosen, at least for the time being, not to return home. A "brain-drain" of this magnitude will have serious consequences for future development. Thus while there are no insurmountable obstacles to the continued modernization of science and technology in China, a change in the political climate and the reestablishment of contacts with the international scientific community, as well as greater investment and reform of the bureaucratic structure, will be necessary for continued success.

Key Concepts

Mutation Theory. In mutation theory, qualitative changes in physical states are related to numerological structures such as hexagrams, as in the *Yijing [I-ching],* or *Book of Changes,* explaining how the elements of the Five Phases (see below) produced each other.

Resonance Theory. Resonance theory is a Daoist concept that explains causation in nature. Daoists believe that the symbolic correlations in all things form one colossal pattern. Things behave in certain ways because their position in the ever-moving cyclical universe endows them with an intrinsic nature that makes their behavior inevitable. Things in the universe that belong to the same class (see the Five Phases below) resonate with, or energize, each other.

Yin-Yang. Yin and *yang* describe perfect opposition within a perfect unity. Anything at any time at any place has a *yin-yang* relationship with some other thing, time, or place. Female is *yin* to male as *yang.* The moon is *yin* to the sun as *yang.* North is *yin* to south as *yang.* This concept of two primal forces or modes of creation first became a major element of Chinese thought during the Han dynasty (202 B.C.–220 A.D.).

Alchemy. Alchemy is a chemical science and speculative philosophy that aims to achieve the transmutation of the base metals into gold, the discovery of a universal cure for disease, and the discovery of a means of prolonging life indefinitely. Alchemy was an important component of Daoism.

Geomancy. Geomancy is a branch of traditional Chinese science that is used to determine the auspicious placement of houses and tombs with respect to features of the landscape.

Five Phases. The Five Phases—wood, fire, metal, water, and earth—are similar in concept to the *yin-yang* theory. Like *yin* and *yang,* the phases are metaphysical forces or modes that dominate or control certain periods of time, commonly the seasons, in a fixed succession. Wood is assigned to the season of spring; fire to summer; metal to autumn; and water to winter. Since there are only four seasons, earth, associated with the color yellow, is commonly assigned a position in the center, aiding the other elements in their governing of the four seasons.

Review Questions

1. What factors retarded the growth of Chinese science in the first half of the twentieth century, according to DeWoskin's Introduction?

2. As discussed in the Sivin article, what were the most common tools of abstract thought in ancient China? What basic understanding of nature did they convey?

3. Give examples of how these traditional "tools" and their underlying concepts affected some of the major scientific disciplines.

4. According to the article by Orleans, what have been China's development priorities since 1949? What does the author conclude are China's two most pressing problems in connection with modernization?

5. What factors does Orleans cite as having impeded China's modernization? How does his explanation compare with DeWoskin's?

6. What advantages to the United States and other developed nations can cooperation with Chinese scientists provide, according to Orleans?

7. In Fang Yi's speech, what were the modernization aims articulated by Chairman Mao and Premier Zhou? What eight spheres does Fang Yi list as most important to the Eight Year Plan for modernizing science and technology?

8. What organizational changes does Fang Yi outline for implementing the policy goals?

9. Why are electronics and computer technology so important to China?

10. What is the status of China's computer industry today, according to Baum?

11. What is the Chinese understanding of the heavens, earth, and humans? What basic concepts express these views?

12. What were some of the major Chinese inventions and discoveries in science, as shown in the video? What were the impediments to China's continued advance in this area?

Essay/Discussion Questions for Part 5

1. Discuss the changing attitudes toward and roles of the arts in China in this century.

Suggested guidelines:

a. Consider the traditional attitudes and roles, referring to:

- DeWoskin's discussion in the Introduction of the role of the arts in imperial China
- the video "Creating," concerning the influence of Daoism, Buddhism, and Confucianism
- the concept of *qi* and the northern and southern schools of landscape painting

b. Review the reform movements in the arts and literature, with reference to:

- DeWoskin's Introduction, regarding the May Fourth Movement, and "Kung I-chi," concerning the movement's attitude toward tradition and literary reform

- Mao's attitude toward tradition and foreign influence, expressed in "Talks at the Yan'an Conference"

- attitudes toward both traditional and modern poetry

- the video "Creating," showing the attitudes of artists concerning Western art and its relation to Chinese art forms

- the new style of reportage exemplified by Liu Binyan

c. Consider the experiences of artists during the Mao and post-Mao years, as revealed in:

- the video "Creating," especially the relationship between artists and politics

- Mao's attitudes toward artists

- the story "The Wounded," and the conflict between individual feelings and loyalties, and political dictates

- the Chinese interest in both indigenous values and Western life

2. What is the traditional Chinese understanding of the relationship between the body and the universe, and how has this shaped traditional medicine in China?

Suggested guidelines:

a. Review the traditional concepts and their applications in the video "Understanding," DeWoskin's Introduction, and Sivin's article, with attention to:

- the concepts of *qi* and *yin-yang*

- the understanding of illness and health

- the attitude toward the earth (refer also to Murphey's "Man and Nature in China" in Part 1)

- the relationships among the body, mind, and nature

3. In his article, Orleans says "The PRC is by no means a typical developing country." Discuss the meaning of this statement with reference to China's history of scientific achievements, the reasons for the decline, and the goals of and obstacles to current policies.

Suggested guidelines:

a. Consider China's long history of discovery and invention, and the reasons for the decline in science, referring to:

- the video "Understanding"
- DeWoskin's discussion in the Introduction

b. Review China's current priorities in science and technology, referring to the articles by Orleans, Fang Yi, and Baum.

c. Consider the enormity of the challenge of scientific modernization, with reference to the impediments to be overcome, as discussed in:

- the Introduction, especially regarding ambivalent attitudes toward foreign involvement
- the Orleans selection on the effects of the Cultural Revolution
- Fang Yi's speech and the implications of deficiencies in institutional structures

Part 6

The Future

Part 6 speculates on likely future developments in China, considering economic, political, and social problems as well as Sino-American relations.

Unit 13: China's Prospects

Video: "Facing the Future: China Approaches the Twenty-First Century"

Readings

Introduction to Part 6, by Steven M. Goldstein

63. "Evolutionary Changes in Chinese Culture," by Martin K. Whyte
64. "The Impact of Tiananmen on the Political Climate of Economic Reform," by Nina Halpern
65. "American Policy after Tiananmen and the Chinese Response," Michael Oksenberg / James Seymour / Winston Lord / Liu Maoyin

Learning Objectives

To become acquainted with:

— political divisions within China's leadership over the process of reform in the 1980s

— tensions among Chinese tradition, Western influences, and Marxism-Leninism in the reformulation of Chinese culture

— elite politics in the aftermath of the Tiananmen Massacre

— debate over the United States' response to the political crackdown in China and the prospects for future Sino-American relations

— official Chinese views of the sources of political dissent and unrest in the 1980s

— the current state of Sino-American relations and prospects for the future

Overview

Throughout this course we have looked at the influence of China's past on its recent, ongoing struggle to modernize. While innovations in political, social, and economic institutions are altering the face of contemporary China, many traditional values and beliefs continue to shape Chinese attitudes and behavior. The readings in Unit 13 look at China's prospects for the future. In the past, Western observers have not had much success in predicting China's future. For example, the Cultural Revolution, which had such an enormous impact on Chinese society, took most outside observers by surprise. Thus, while all predictions of China's future remain tentative at best, this unit provides some educated guesses as to what the future might hold for China.

Throughout the the 1980s American observers almost universally applauded China's political and economic reforms. As China's leaders struggled to push reform forward, expectations rose both at home and abroad. The unprecedented and largely peaceful changes that swept Eastern Europe during the late 1980s further encouraged the rosy forecasts for China's economic and political development. Consequently, the brutal crackdown on political dissent on June 4, 1989, stunned the world and continues to cast a pall over China's future. Steven Goldstein's Introduction to Part 6 offers three possible scenarios for China's development in the 1990s, which range from civil war to renewed efforts at reform. One common thread in these disparate projections is the continued importance of elite political struggles in determining China's future.

As the tragic events of June 1989 demonstrated, ultimately elite politics are more decisive than popular protest. Almost since the economic reforms began in 1978 there have been important differences of opinion among Chinese leaders concerning the pace and direction of reform. Official corruption, price inflation, and consumer discontent had seriously begun to erode the consensus for reform as early as 1988. Nevertheless, despite the forceful military crackdown and the apparent unity of China's more conservative leaders, a consensus on the future course of economic and political development has yet to emerge. As Halpern convincingly argues in her essay, in the aftermath of the Tiananmen Incident, conservative elements led by Li Peng have been able to effect personnel changes, launch a media campaign to discredit reformers, and reestablish political control over the population, but so far the conservative leadership has yet to articulate an attractive or original alternative to the previous decade of reform.

Cultural ambiguity is the subject of Martin Whyte's essay, which takes a much broader look at China's problems in the 1980s. According to Whyte, the Chinese must come to grips with three cultural alternatives—traditional Chinese customs and values, Marxist-Leninist practices, and Western influences—in order to define and develop a new cultural orthodoxy. When the Communist Party relaxed its grip on literature, the arts, and the mass media during the 1980s, the result was the revival of many aspects of traditional Chinese culture as well as the introduction of a wide array of foreign influences on both high and low culture. Based on what Whyte considers the historically rooted Chinese need for cultural consensus, the revival of tradition and the simultaneous influx of foreign culture have produced an unsettling condition of cultural ambiguity that has had a broad impact on Chinese society.

With few exceptions, the international community expressed deep disgust at the bloody events of June 1989. Most Americans were shocked and outraged by the senseless killings, and many were disappointed with President Bush's response. The articles by Oksenberg, Seymour, and Lord illustrate the dimensions of the debate over the United States' reaction to the Tiananmen Massacre. In light of China's geopolitical importance and with an eye to the long-term Sino-American relationship, Oksenberg supports the Bush administration's limited response and argues for continued restraint. Seymour acknowledges the relevant geopolitical considerations, but, under the circumstances that he carefully outlines, advocates stronger sanctions to establish a moral stance against serious human rights violations. Writing approximately one year after the Tiananmen Incident, former ambassador Lord takes up the question of granting most-favored-nation trading status (MFN) to China. Lord proposes an explicit linkage between human rights and trade. In this way, Lord seeks to counteract the impression that hard-line leaders in China may have received given the double standard that the Bush administration applied between China and the support for democracy in Eastern Europe. On the other hand, Lord is well aware that the suspension of MFN could do serious harm to the people of China. Given the emotional impact of the Tiananmen Massacre and the failure of the current regime to acknowledge human rights violations, maintaining a balance between moral, economic, and political considerations undoubtedly will remain difficult.

Liu Maoyin's call to arms against the ideological infiltration and economic inducements of the bourgeoisie and reactionaries of the West is revealing in several ways. What most Americans consider to be positive developments in Sino-American relations are denounced in Liu's highly polemical statement. According to Liu, the increasing trade and cultural contacts with the West are actually part of a "sinister and ruthless" strategy to undermine socialism in China and elsewhere. Liu's polemic is reminiscent of the Cultural Revolution in China, but it also has a disturbing resonance with McCarthyism in the United States during the 1950s. Employing language of the Cold War era, Liu resurrects images of a world locked in struggle between capitalism and socialism.

Clearly, Liu's arguments are also designed to garner political support for the post-Tiananmen political leadership. Nevertheless, his statement does not bode well for American observers' hope that the "peaceful evolution" denounced by Liu will resume. By identifying all foreign influences as pernicious threats to Chinese socialism, Liu attempts to manipulate Chinese xenophobia for short-term political gains. This situation is far from encouraging, but, as Goldstein noted in the Introduction, predicting China's future is a hazardous task. Elite politics remain important in the short term; popular movements could reemerge eventually; many economic problems remain unsolved; and contacts with the West may be curtailed. It remains to be seen if the events of 1989 were an isolated incident or the prelude to a new epoch in Chinese history.

In the video "Facing the Future," a panel of experts offer their opinions on China's future. Martin Whyte notes that an enormous population and continued resistance to the one-child policy threaten to dilute the benefits of economic growth, while the failed promises of reform have disillusioned many Chinese, particularly educated youth. Reforms in the work-place have undermined the security of workers, as Margaret Pearson notes, while Stanley Lubman observes that foreign investors remain wary due to China's fragile legal system. In the political realm, Steven Goldstein points out that since 1949 the transfer of political power has never been smooth. Furthermore, given the advanced age of China's leaders, change is inevitable, and leaders who advocated reform, although temporarily eclipsed, have survived and might yet stage a comeback. Finally, Rhoads Murphey reminds us that broad generalizations are problematic given the geographic and ethnic diversity of China.

Review Questions

1. What are the four factors influencing politics at the leadership level that, Goldstein argues, indicate a turning point in the development of post-Mao China?

2. What are the three possible scenarios for China's future outlined in the video "Facing the Future"? In terms of conflicts within the political

leadership, how do these scenarios compare with Halpern's assessment?

3. What are the three distinct cultural alternatives under contention in Chinese society, according to Whyte's essay in Unit 13?

4. What has been the three-part agenda of the Chinese leadership in the aftermath of the Tiananmen Incident, according to Halpern? How successfully has this agenda been carried out?

5. To what does Halpern attribute the lack of political consensus in China since the Tiananmen Incident?

6. What are the important geopolitical considerations that Oksenberg feels should inform Sino-American relations after the Tiananmen Massacre?

7. How does Seymour's long-term view of Sino-American relations differ from the views of Oksenberg and Lord?

8. What criteria does Seymour propose to guide the use of economic sanctions against China?

9. In former ambassador Lord's opinion, how should the United States use the granting of most-favored-nation status to influence China's leaders?

10. What does Liu Maoyin mean by a "smokeless war"? What are the five principal tactics of the smokeless war, as identified by Liu?

Essay/Discussion Questions for Part 6

1. How do the authors of this final unit evaluate the future of China's political and economic development?

Suggested guidelines:

a. Consider the pitfalls of Chinese "futurology" discussed by Goldstein in the Introduction.

b. Review the importance of elite politics in determining the direction of economic and political reforms, referring to Halpern's article.

c. Examine the historical importance of official ideology and cultural identity in China. Consider the relative importance of the three cultural "alternatives" that Whyte identifies.

d. Compare the various American responses to the event at Tiananmen. Can moral concerns and geopolitical interests be balanced? What options are available to the United States government?

e. Compare the optimistic, pessimistic, and middle-ground scenarios offered in the video "Facing the Future."

f. How effective can any foreigners be in influencing Chinese politics? Think about Liu Maoyin's assessment of Western influences on Chinese society.

Appendices

The pinyin system of romanization, adopted in the People's Republic of China after 1949, has increasingly replaced the older Wade-Giles system in contemporary Western writings on China. Students will encounter both forms in *The Chinese*. The highly simplified chart in Appendix 1 will help students pronounce Chinese words spelled in pinyin. Appendix 2 will help them recognize alternative spellings of the names of persons, places, and things.

Appendix 1: Pinyin Pronunciation Guide

In pinyin letters have approximately the same sounds as in English, with the following exceptions:

Consonants

c: sounds like the ts in *its*
q: sounds like the ch in *China*
x: sounds like the sh in *shell*
zh: sounds like the j in *jump*

Vowels

e: sounds like the e in talent
e: when directly before ng, e sounds like the u in *lung*
o: sounds like the aw in *saw*
ou: sounds like the o in *go*

Appendix 2: Pinyin/Wade-Giles Conversion Chart

Pinyin	*Wade-Giles*	*Pinyin*	*Wade-Giles*
a	a	chan	ch'an
ai	ai	chang	ch'ang
an	an	chao	ch'ao
ang	ang	che	ch'e
ao	ao	chen	ch'eng
ba	pa	chi	ch'ih
bai	pai	chong	ch'ung
ban	pan	chou	ch'ou
bang	pang	chu	ch'u
bao	pao	chuai	ch'uai
bei	pei	chuan	ch'uan
ben	pen	chuang	ch'uang
beng	peng	chui	ch'ui
bi	pi	chun	ch'un
bian	pien	chuo	ch'o
biao	piao	ci	tz'u
bie	pieh	cong	ts'ung
bin	pin	cou	ts'ou
bing	ping	cu	ts'u
bo	po	cuan	ts'uan
bou	pou	cui	ts'ui
bu	pu	cun	ts'un
ca	ts'a	cuo	ts'o
cai	ts'ai	da	ta
can	ts'an	dai	tai
cang	ts'ang	dan	tan
cao	ts'ao	dang	tang
ce	ts'e	dao	tao
cen	ts'en	de	te
ceng	ts'eng	dei	tei
cha	ch'a	di	ti
chai	ch'ai	dian	tien

Pinyin	***Wade-Giles***	***Pinyin***	***Wade-Giles***
diao	tiao	gu	ku
die	tieh	gua	kua
ding	ting	guai	kuai
diu	tiu	guan	kuan
dong	tung	guang	kuang
dou	tou	gui	kuei
du	tu	gun	kun
duan	tuan	guo	kuo
dui	tui	ha	ha
dun	tun	hai	hai
duo	to	han	han
e	e, o	hang	hang
ei	ei	hao	hao
en	en	he	he,ho
eng	eng	hei	hei
er	erh	hen	hen
fa	fa	heng	heng
fan	fan	hong	hung
fang	fang	hou	hou
fei	fei	hu	hu
fen	fen	hua	hua
feng	feng	huai	huai
fo	fo	huan	huan
fou	fou	huang	huang
fu	fu	hui	hui
ga	ka	hun	hun
gai	kai	huo	huo
gan	kan	ji	chi
gao	kao	jia	chia
ge	ke, ko	jian	chien
gei	kei	jiang	chiang
gen	ken	jiao	chiao
geng	keng	jie	chieh
gong	kung	jin	chin
gou	kou	jing	ching

Pinyin	Wade-Giles	Pinyin	Wade-Giles
jiong	chiung	liao	liao
jiu	chiu	lie	lieh
ju	chü	lin	lin
juan	chüan	ling	ling
jue	chüeh	liu	liu
jun	chün	long	lung
ka	k'a	lou	lou
kai	k'ai	lu	lu
kan	k'an	luan	luan
kao	k'ao	lun	lun
ke	k'e, k'o	luo	lo
ken	k'en	lü	lü
keng	k'eng	lüe	lüeh
kong	k'ung	ma	ma
kou	k'ou	mai	mai
ku	k'u	man	man
kua	k'ua	mang	mang
kuai	k'uai	mao	mao
kuan	k'uan	mei	mei
kuang	k'uang	men	men
kui	k'uei	meng	meng
kun	k'un	mi	mi
kuo	k'uo	mian	mien
la	la	miao	miao
lai	lai	mie	mieh
lan	lan	min	min
lang	lang	ming	ming
lao	lao	miu	miu
le	le	mo	mo
lei	lei	mou	mou
leng	leng	mu	mu
li	li	na	na
lia	lia	nai	nai
lian	lien	nan	nan
liang	liang	nang	nang

Pinyin	Wade-Giles	Pinyin	Wade-Giles
nao	nao	ping	p'ing
ne	ne	pu	pu
nei	nei	qi	ch'i
nen	nen	qia	ch'ia
neng	neng	qian	ch'ien
nong	nung	qiang	ch'iang
nou	nou	qiao	ch'iao
ni	ni	qie	ch'ieh
nian	nien	qin	ch'in
niang	niang	qing	ch'ing
niao	niao	qiong	ch'iung
nie	nieh	qiu	ch'iu
nin	nin	qu	ch'ü
ning	ning	quan	ch'üan
niu	niu	que	ch'üeh
nu	nu	qun	ch'ün
nuan	nuan	ran	jan
nuo	no	rang	jang
nü	nü	rao	jao
nue	nüeh	re	je
pa	p'a	ren	jen
pai	p'ai	reng	jeng
pan	p'an	ri	jih
pang	p'ang	rong	jung
pao	p'ao	rou	jou
pei	p'ei	ru	ju
pen	p'en	ruan	juan
peng	p'eng	rui	jui
po	p'o	run	jun
pou	p'ou	ruo	jo
pi	p'i	sa	sa
pian	p'ien	sai	sai
piao	p'iao	san	san
pie	p'ieh	sang	sang
pin	p'in	sao	sao

Pinyin	Wade-Giles	Pinyin	Wade-Giles
se	se	te	t'e
sen	sen	teng	t'eng
seng	seng	ti	t'i
sha	sha	tian	t'ien
shai	shai	tiao	t'iao
shan	shan	tie	t'ieh
shang	shang	ting	t'ing
shao	shao	tong	t'ung
she	she	tou	t'ou
shei	shei	tu	t'u
shen	shen	tuan	t'uan
sheng	sheng	tui	t'ui
shi	shih	tun	t'un
shou	shou	tuo	t'o
shu	shu	wa	wa
shua	shua	wai	wai
shuai	shuai	wan	wan
shuan	shuan	wang	wang
shuang	shuang	wei	wei
shui	shui	wen	wen
shun	shun	weng	weng
shuo	shuo	wo	wo
si	szu	wu	wu
song	sung	xi	hsi
sou	sou	xia	hsia
su	su	xian	hsien
suan	suan	xiang	hsiang
sui	sui	xiao	hsiao
sun	sun	xie	hsieh
suo	so	xin	hsin
ta	t'a	xing	hsing
tai	t'ai	xiong	hsiung
tan	t'an	xiu	hsiu
tang	t'ang	xu	hsü
tao	t'ao	xuan	hsüan

Pinyin	Wade-Giles	Pinyin	Wade-Giles
xue	hsüeh	zhan	chan
xun	hsün	zhang	chang
ya	ya	zhao	chao
yan	yen	zhe	che
yang	yang	zhei	chei
yao	yao	zhen	chen
ye	yeh	zheng	cheng
yi	i	zhi	chih
yin	yin	zhong	chung
ying	ying	zhou	chou
yong	yung	zhu	chu
you	yu	zhua	chua
yu	yü	zhuai	chuai
yuan	yüan	zhuan	chuan
yue	yüeh	zhuang	chuang
yun	yün	zhui	chui
za	tsa	zhun	chun
zai	tsai	zhuo	cho
zan	tsan	zi	tzu
zang	tsang	zong	tsung
zao	tsao	zou	tsou
ze	tse	zu	tsu
zei	tsei	zuan	tsuan
zen	tsen	zui	tsui
zeng	tseng	zun	tsun
zha	cha	zuo	tso
zhai	chai		